TREKKING THE GR11 TRAIL

THE TRAVERSE OF THE SPANISH PYRENEES
- LA SENDA PIRENAICA

by Tom Martens

JUNIPER HOUSE, MURLEY MOSS,
OXENHOLME ROAD, KENDAL, CUMBRIA LA9 7RL
www.cicerone.co.uk

© Tom Martens 2024
Seventh edition 2024
ISBN: 978 1 78631 166 5
Sixth edition 2018
Fifth edition 2014
Fourth edition 2008
Third Edition 2004
Second Edition 2000
First Edition 1996

Printed in Czechia on behalf of Latitude Press Ltd on responsibly sourced paper.
A catalogue record for this book is available from the British Library.

Route mapping by Lovell Johns www.lovelljohns.com
All photographs are by the author unless otherwise stated.
Contains OpenStreetMap.org data © OpenStreetMap contributors, CC-BY-SA. NASA relief data courtesy of ESRI

Updates to this guide

While every effort is made by our authors to ensure the accuracy of guidebooks as they go to print, changes can occur during the lifetime of an edition. Any updates that we know of for this guide will be on the Cicerone website (www.cicerone.co.uk/1166/updates), so please check before planning your trip. We also advise that you check information about such things as transport, accommodation and shops locally. Even rights of way can be altered over time.

We are always grateful for information about any discrepancies between a guidebook and the facts on the ground, sent by email to updates@cicerone.co.uk or by post to Cicerone, Juniper House, Murley Moss, Oxenholme Road, Kendal, LA9 7RL.

Register your book: To sign up to receive free updates, special offers and GPX files where available, create a Cicerone account and register your purchase via the 'My Account' tab at www.cicerone.co.uk.

Front cover: Hikers near Port de Caldes in the Aigüestortes i Estany de Sant Maurici national parc

CONTENTS

Note on mapping

The route maps in this guide are derived from publicly available data, databases and crowd-sourced data. As such they have not been through the detailed checking procedures that would generally be applied to a published map from an official mapping agency. However, we have reviewed them closely in light of local knowledge as part of the preparation of this guide.

Hiker near Lac deth Cap de Pòrt (Stage 24A)

Symbols used on route maps

Symbol	Meaning	Symbol	Meaning
~	route	⊕	airport
~	alternative stage	P	parking
~~-	variant route	◓	accommodation
Ⓢ	start point	🍴	refreshments
Ⓕ	finish point	⛺	campsite
ⓢⓕ	start/finish point	⊕	shop
Ⓢ	alternative start point	𝒊	information
Ⓕ	alternative finish point	⬙	tap water/spring
	glacier		
	woodland		
	urban areas		
	international border		
—◉—	station/railway		
▲	peak		
⤳	pass		
⬆⌂	manned/unmanned hut		
■	building		
=	bridge		

Relief
in metres

3250–3500
3000–3250
2750–3000
2500–2750
2250–2500
2000–2250
1750–2000
1500–1750
1250–1500
1000–1250
750–1000
500–750
250–500
0–250

SCALE: 1:100,000

0 kilometres 1 2
0 miles 1

Contour lines are drawn at 50m intervals and highlighted at 200m intervals.

GPX files

GPX files for all routes can be downloaded for free at www.cicerone.co.uk/1166.

ROUTE SUMMARY TABLE

Stage	Start	Finish
Cabo de Higuer – Zuriza		
1	Cabo de Higuer	Bera
2	Bera	Elizondo
3	Elizondo	Puerto de Urkiaga
4	Puerto de Urkiaga	Burguete
5	Burguete	Hiriberri
6	Hiriberri	Ochagavía
7	Ochagavía	Isaba
8	Isaba	Zuriza
8A	Isaba	Zuriza (via Peña Ezkaurri, GR11.4)
Zuriza – Parzán		
9	Zuriza	La Mina (GR11)
9A	Zuriza	Puente de Santa Ana (GR11.1)
10	La Mina	Refugio de Lizara (GR11)
10A	Puente de Santa Ana	Refugio de Lizara (GR11.1)
11	Refugio de Lizara	Candanchú
12	Candanchú	Sallent de Gállego
13	Sallent de Gállego	Refugio de Respomuso
14	Refugio de Respomuso	Baños de Panticosa
15	Baños de Panticosa	San Nicolás de Bujaruelo
16	San Nicolás de Bujaruelo	Refugio de Góriz
17	Refugio de Góriz	Refugio de Pineta (GR11)
17A	Refugio de Góriz	Refugio de Pineta (GR11.9)
18	Refugio de Pineta	Parzán
Parzán – La Guingueta d'Àneu		
19	Parzán	Refugio de Biadós
20	Refugio de Biadós	Puente de San Jaime
20A	Refugio de Biadós	Refugio d'Ángel Orús (GR11.2)
20B	Refugio d'Ángel Orús	Puente de San Jaime (GR11.2)
21	Puente de San Jaime	Refugio de Cap de Llauset
22	Refugio de Cap de Llauset	Refugi de Conangles

High point and passes	Distance	Ascent	Descent	Time	Page
Collado de Erlaitz (448m), Collado de Tellería (415m)	31.4km	830m	820m	8hr 30min	45
Santa Bárbara (396m), Collado Achuela (795m)	30.1km	1270m	1120m	8hr 20min	50
Collado Bustalmorro (1170m)	17.6km	1090m	395m	5hr 20min	55
Collado Aratun (1212m), Menditxipi (1213m)	17.2km	765m	780m	5hr 10min	59
Ridge below Latxaga (1185m)	17.4km	695m	670m	4hr 45min	63
Abodi Occidental Idorrokia (1492m), Muskilda (1071m)	20.6km	820m	970m	6hr 50min	66
Collado de Saitsederra (1363m)	19.1km	675m	635m	5hr 20min	71
Collau d'Arguibiela (1295m)	10.8km	595m	180m	2hr 50min	74
Peña Ezkaurri (2047m)	16.7km	1390m	970m	7hr	77
Cuella Petrafiche (1964m)	11.5km	840m	820m	4hr 10min	82
Cuello d'Estribiella (1992m)	18.3km	1050m	1340m	6hr 15min	85
Col north of Punta Alta d'a Portaza (1909m), Puerto de Bernera (2115m)	20.2km	1170m	860m	6hr 45min	87
Cuello de lo Foratón (2016m)	12km	1175m	555m	4hr 45min	91
Puerto de Aisa (2262m), Paso de Tuca Blanca (2207m)	14.8km	1060m	1030m	5hr 55min	94
Ibón d'Anayet (2227m)	23.9km	905m	1180m	6hr 40min	97
Refugio de Respomuso (2220m)	11.1km	955m	30m	3hr 55min	102
Collado de Tebarray (Piedrafita) (2765m), Collado del Infierno (2721m)	12.4km	715m	1300m	6hr 20	105
Collado Alta de Brazato (2566m)	19.9km	930m	1225m	7hr 15min	109
Refugio de Góriz (2160m)	24.3km	1270m	450m	7hr 55min	113
Collado de Añisclo (2453m)	12.8km	1135m	2055m	7hr 20min	118
SE ridge of Punta de las Olas (2700m)	11.7km	600m	1520m	6hr 20min	121
Collado las Coronetas (2159m)	19.5km	1370m	1480m	6hr	123
Collado de Urdiceto (2314m)	21.1km	1520	890m	7hr	130
Puerto de Chistau (2572m)	20.1km	940m	1450m	6hr 45min	134
Collada Eriste (2864m)	10.2km	1195m	840m	5hr 35min	138
Collada de la Plana (2702m)	13.9km	720m	1585m	6hr 10min	140
Collado de Ballibierna (2732m)	16.9km	1570m	395m	7hr 10min	142
Collet dels Estanyets (2524m)	10km	240m	1110m	3hr 45min	145

Stage	Start	Finish
23	Refugi de Conangles	Refugi dera Restanca
24	Refugi dera Restanca	Refugi de Colomèrs (GR11)
24A	Refugi dera Restanca	Refugi de Colomèrs (via Port de Caldes, GR11.18)
25	Refugi de Colomèrs	Espot
26	Espot	La Guingueta d'Àneu
La Guingueta d'Àneu – Puigcerdà		
27	La Guingueta d'Àneu	Estaon
28	Estaon	Tavascan
29	Tavascan	Àreu
30	Àreu	Refugi de Vallferrera
31	Refugi de Vallferrera	Refugi de Comapedrosa
32	Refugi de Comapedrosa	Arans
33	Arans	Encamp
34	Encamp	Refugio de l'Illa
35	Refugio de l'Illa	Refugi de Malniu
36	Refugi de Malniu	Puigcerdà
Puigcerdà – Cap de Creus		
37	Puigcerdà	Camping Can Fosses
38	Camping Can Fosses	Núria
39	Núria	Setcases
40	Setcases	Beget
41	Beget	San Aniol d'Aguja
42	San Aniol d'Aguja	Albanyà
43	Albanyà	Maçanet de Cabrenys
44	Maçanet de Cabrenys	La Jonquera
45	La Jonquera	Els Vilars
46	Els Vilars	Llançà (GR11)
46A	Els Vilars	Llançà (via Espolla and Rabós)
47	Llançà	Cap de Creus

High point and passes	Distance	Ascent	Descent	Time	Page
Pòrt de Rius (2355m)	12km	970m	515m	5hr 20min	148
Coret d'Oelhacrestada (2475m)	13.9km	985m	860m	5hr 5min	151
Coret d'Oelhacrestada (2475m), Port de Caldes (2570m)	7.1km	695m	565m	3hr 50min	153
Pòrt de Ratèra (2590m)	19km	525m	1330m	6hr	155
Estaís (1400m)	9.7km	250m	600m	2hr 30min	160
Coll de Montcaubo (2201m)	11.3km	1280m	1000m	5hr 35min	166
Coll de Jou (1830m)	12.8km	730m	850m	4hr 15min	169
Coll de Tudela (2243m)	16.7km	1245m	1095m	6hr 30min	172
Refugi de Vallferrera (1920m)	10km	740m	90m	3hr 20min	175
Portella de Baiau (2757m)	10.4km	1000m	660m	5hr 20min	177
Refugi de Comapedrosa (2260m), Coll de les Cases (1958m)	9.7km	535m	1435m	4hr	180
Coll d'Ordino (1983m)	14.9km	1085m	1175m	6hr	183
Coll Jovell (1779m), Refugio de l'Illa (2485m)	15.8km	1370m	155m	5hr 45min	187
Coll de Vall Civera (2550m), Portella d'Engorgs (2680m)	14.3km	780m	1125m	5hr 35min	190
North slope of Planell de l'Agulla (2217m)	14.2km	95m	1030m	3hr 10min	194
Coll de Marcer (1980m), Coll de la Creu de Meians (2000m)	27.1km	1055m	1000m	6hr 50min	202
Collet de les Barraques (1890m), Creu d'en Riba (1983m)	18.2km	1475m	770m	6hr 25min	206
Coll de Tirapits (2780m), Col de Noucreus (2785m), Coll de la Marrana (2520m)	19.7km	1045m	1745m	6hr	211
Summit above Coll de Lliens (1904m)	23.3km	810m	1535m	6hr 20min	215
Coll dels Muls (700m), Talaixà (760m)	15.7km	750m	840m	4hr 25min	219
Coll Roig (840m), Coll de Principi (1126m)	18.2km	785m	995m	5hr 10min	222
East ridge, Puig de la Trilla (690m)	19.7km	780m	670m	4hr 45min	227
Puig de la Creu (600m)	23.1km	555m	790m	5hr 10min	231
Puig dels Falguers (778m), Coll de la Llosarda (690m)	25.1km	995m	890m	6hr 35min	234
Coll de la Plaja (395m), Coll de la Serra (260m), Coll de les Portes (230m)	26.1km	565m	790m	5hr 30min	238
Col de la Serra (260m)	20.5km	420m	630m	4hr 35min	242
Santa Pere de Rodes (500m)	27.7km	1015m	1015m	7hr 35min	245

Belgian hiker at Ibones Altos de los Batanes with the Vignemale (3298m) behind (Stage 15)

Mountain safety

Every mountain walk has its dangers, and those described in this guidebook are no exception. All who walk or climb in the mountains should recognise this and take responsibility for themselves and their companions along the way. The author and publisher have made every effort to ensure that the information contained in this guide was correct when it went to press, but, except for any liability that cannot be excluded by law, they cannot accept responsibility for any loss, injury or inconvenience sustained by any person using this book.

International distress signal *(emergency only)*
Six blasts on a whistle (and flashes with a torch after dark) spaced evenly for one minute, followed by a minute's pause. Repeat until an answer is received. The response is three signals per minute followed by a minute's pause.

Helicopter rescue
The following signals are used to communicate with a helicopter:

Help needed: raise both arms above head to form a 'Y'

Help not needed: raise one arm above head, extend other arm downward

Emergency telephone numbers
112 or 062 for the Guardia Civil
(Civil Guard - for mountain rescue services and other accidents)

Weather reports
www.meteo.cat
www.meteoblue.com
www.mountain-forecast.com

Mountain rescue can be very expensive – be adequately insured.

On the way down to Estanys Cap d'Angliós (Stage 22)

PREFACE

There are amazing hiking trails in Europe and for me the GR11 is definitely one of them. It fits into a select group of long-distance hikes through beautiful, impressive natural scenery, and at the same time it offers glimpses of the cultural diversity of the Spanish Pyrenees.

Over the years the GR11 has become a well-defined hiking trail which mostly goes over good hiking paths through largely unspoilt and wild mountains. Especially in Navarre, new efforts have been made to reduce road walking to a minimum and overall the waymarking has improved significantly. On an 850km trail it is inevitable that waymark maintenance is needed in some places, but in general you will very easily stay on track.

The first Cicerone guide to the GR11 was published back in 1996, when the route was still ill-defined with little waymarking. Continuous improvements along the trail kept first Paul Lucia and later Brian Johnson busy updating the GR11 guide. I'd like to praise both inspiring hiker-writers, whose work I am now continuing with a feeling of modesty.

This new edition is of course again a comprehensive practical guidebook, and in addition to that the reader with an interest in wildlife, flowers and culture will find a preview of what is to be experienced out there.

On solo hikes in the Pyrenees one often meets other hikers and my own GR11 hike was no exception. I'd like to thank all the hikers I met on the way, in particular Marie, with whom I teamed up a week into the trail and continued most of the way until the Mediterranean Sea. Her great outdoor spirit and knowledge of the Catalan language added extra colour to an already fantastic adventure.

Ibones d'Anayet with a view on Pic du Midi d'Ossau (Stage 12)

PUBLISHER'S DEDICATION

After the death of Paul Lucia, the mantle of taking on Cicerone's GR11 guidebook passed to the indomitable Brian Johnson, a bearded trekker with an penchant for ultra-long trails. Not only did Brian revise and write the GR11 guide, but he also authored guides to the GR10, the Corbetts, the epic Pacific Crest Trail (which he walked numerous times) and the wonderful Shorter Treks in the Pyrenees.

Orienteering was one of Brian's passions. After racing at a high level when younger, he came back to the sport to compete in the Masters classifications at various orienteering championships across Europe. Brian was also a true sporting polymath too. He was a climber, cyclist and cricketer, a player of hockey, bridge, bowls and chess; he won the 1995/96 World Amateur Chess Championships.

My thanks to David Johnson for agreeing to let us build on Brian's work, and we are thrilled that dedicated Pyreneeist Tom Martens is now responsible for Cicerone's GR11 guide. As we have said before, thanks must also go to the many Cicerone trekkers whose comments have helped the GR11 and our guides to the route go from strength to strength.

Joe Williams, Cicerone Press, March 2024

Lac Redon and Lac Long (Stage 25) (photo: Brian Johnson)

INTRODUCTION

In recent years there has been a growing interest in long-distance hiking in the Pyrenees. The impressive and tranquil mountain landscape, dotted with lakes, is seeing good numbers of enthusiasts without becoming too crowded. It is this unique combination of picturesque scenery and peacefulness which draws hikers to the mountain chain. Many come for a couple of weeks, while others are lucky enough to have the time to do a long-distance trail in one season. A smaller group of avid hikers have become so fascinated with the Pyrenees that they spend several weeks there each summer.

As the crow flies, the Pyrenees stretch a little over 400km from the Atlantic Ocean to the Mediterranean Sea, but a long-distance hiker goes about 800km from one side of the mountain chain to the other. In between the two extremities, there are magnificent landscapes with a variety of trails. The GR11 is one of the trails which crosses the whole Pyrenees, staying on the Spanish side of the border, which is marked by the Pyrenees. It provides a very varied and scenic route through magnificent, high mountains, which are often remote and deserted.

The GR11 first goes from the Atlantic Ocean through the border town of Irún and into the green Basque Country. It passes over gentle grassy and wooded hills, visiting authentic villages on the way. On day six, the hills have made way for modest limestone mountains. A week and a half into the trail you get a first taste of the High Pyrenees, near Candanchú. The scenery becomes more and more impressive as you go by the Balaïtous (the first 3000er in the western Pyrenees) at Respomuso. Further on, as you approach the world-renowned Ordesa and Monte Perdido National Park, there's colourful scenery with steep canyons carved into Europe's highest limestone massif. Here snowfields on the trail sometimes survive into the first weeks of summer, and you can get a view of the remnants of the huge glaciers which carved out the deep valleys. In the third week on the trail, you hike next to the brown-grey granite Posets (3375m, the second highest peak in the Pyrenees) and through the Maladeta massif. Another national park is reached at the beginning of the fourth week, when you hike into the magnificent Parc Nacional d'Aigüestortes i Estany de Sant Maurici, with its jagged peaks and large waterfalls. The rough mountain landscapes continue into Andorra, after which you cross the plains of Cerdanya. Surprisingly, the GR11 only reaches its highest point when you reach the eastern Pyrenees, near the Núria monastery. The trail then follows a line of wooded hills to finally reach the Mediterranean Sea at the beautiful peninsula of Cap de Creus.

17

GEOLOGY

There haven't always been mountains where the Pyrenees now stretch over 430km from the Atlantic Ocean to the Mediterranean Sea. The geological history of the area sheds light on why we now find complex layers of mainly granite and limestone here. In the early Paleozoic era, 500 million years ago, there was an ocean in the place where we now find the mountain chain. About 400 million years ago, tectonic movement compressed the sedimentary rock that had formed on the ocean bed and began forming a gigantic structure: the Hercynian mountain chain. Eventually there grew a range with peaks as high as today's Himalaya. However, over millions of years the entire Hercynian mountain chain eroded, leaving only the migmatite foot of the chain behind. During much of the Mesozoic era, between 250 and 100 million years ago, the area was covered by a shallow sea, resulting in new layers of sedimentary rock. In the Cretaceous era, around 75 million years ago, a tectonic movement took place that shaped the early Pyrenees: the African plate pushed the Iberian crust (now Spain and Portugal) north, where it began crashing into the huge European crust. This process continued until well into the Cenozoic era, 20 million years ago, and formed the Pyrenean mountain chain.

Different forms of erosion have altered the Pyrenees into the shape we can now see. During long periods with a warm and humid climate, rainfall eroded the rock and transported billions of tons of debris down the rivers, forming valleys along the way. Some 200,000 years ago the temperatures fell drastically and snow piled up extremely high in the valleys. The long glaciers that were created nibbled at the mountains and widened the valleys. Finally, from 5000 years ago, fluvial erosion started again, creating open, steep-sided valleys and gorges.

A few geological highlights along the GR11 are: (from west to east) Cretaceous flysch sedentary rock at Cabo de Higuer, limestone karst landscapes around Peña Ezkaurri, Europe's largest canyons and the highest limestone massif in the Ordesa y Monte Perdido National Park, the dark granite mass of the Posets and the unique limestone formations plunging into the Mediterranean Sea at Cap de Creus.

NATIONAL AND NATURAL PARKS

The GR11 passes through two national parks and six natural parks:
- Parque Natural Aiako Harria
- Parque Natural de Los Valles Occidentales
- Parque Nacional de Ordesa y Monte Perdido
- Parque Natural de Posets-Maladeta
- Parc Nacional d'Aigüestortes i Estany de Sant Maurici
- Parc Natural Alt Pirineu

- Parc Natural Valls de Comapedrosa
- Parc Natural Cap de Creus

The Aiako Harria Natural Parc is crossed in Pais Vasco (Basque Country) through a beautiful forest.

The Valles Occidentales (western valleys) of Aragón are predominantly composed of limestone and are a relatively gentle introduction to the tough alpine terrain ahead of you.

Ordesa and Monte Perdido, a UNESCO World Heritage site, is the largest limestone massif in Western Europe. The highest peak is Monte Perdido (3355m) but it is the deep valleys, with thundering cascades and waterfalls edged by towering limestone, which attract most hikers.

Posets-Maladeta is a granite massif containing half the 3000m summits in the Pyrenees including Aneto (3404m), the highest mountain in the Pyrenees. Glaciated granite mountains provide some of the most spectacular mountain scenery in the world with hundreds of little sparkling lakes nestling in a landscape dominated by bare rock.

As you pass into Catalonia, you pass through the Aigüestortes and Sant Maurici National Park, another magical granite massif, and then the Parc Natural Alt Pirineu, the largest natural park in Catalonia. Alt Pirineu continues into Andorra as the Parc Natural Valls de Comapedrosa.

The GR11 ends with the Parc Natural Cap de Creus, which is a complete contrast: a rocky dry region on a peninsula sticking out into the Mediterranean Sea.

Lac Obago in the Aigüestortes i Estany de Sant Maurici National Park (Stage 25)

FROM THE ATLANTIC TO THE MEDITERRANEAN

There are three long-distance paths along the Pyrenees from the Atlantic to the Mediterranean:

- GR10
- Pyrenean Haute Route (Haute Randonnée Pyrénéenne, HRP)
- GR11 (La Senda Pirenaica)

The oldest and most popular of these routes is the GR10, which is entirely in France. This well-way-marked path is not as high and rough as the GR11 but it passes through equally spectacular terrain. Frequent visits to towns and villages mean accommodation and supplies are easily found. Staying to the north of the watershed, the GR10 has a much cooler and cloudier climate than the GR11.

The HRP, which passes through France, Spain and Andorra, is not waymarked as such, and there are only markers in places where it coincides with other routes. There is plenty of rough terrain, including some very steep descents. Hikers spend a lot of time on high mountain ridges. Accommodation and supplies are sometimes harder to find. The HRP can be an intimidating route for the inexperienced but it is a magnificent expedition for those with the right experience.

The GR11 is a well-waymarked route which passes through Spain and Andorra. Like the HRP, it crosses many high mountain passes where there are boulderfields, scree and

some easy scrambling at about the maximum difficulty the inexperienced hiker would want when carrying a backpack. The weather tends to be considerably sunnier and drier than on the GR10 and thunderstorms are less of an issue than on the HRP as you don't spend long periods on high ridges. Frequent visits to towns and villages mean that resupply is easy. Those who prefer not to camp or bivouac will find that a few of the days are rather long and that some of the alternative routes featured in this guide will need to be taken. There could be issues with snow early in the season, but not later in the summer. Although the GR11 stays considerably higher than the GR10, there is actually considerably less climbing. The GR11 is more challenging than the GR10 as it takes you into tougher terrain, but they are both magnificent walks.

THE GR11

The total route is about 850km long with 43,000m of ascent and is described here in 47 stages. Geographically, it can be broken down into three broad regions.

- The first eight stages go through the lower and more verdant Basque Country and Navarre, offering a gentle warming up for the higher stages ahead. These stages allow for a fast pace, and hikers will cover 165km in 8 stages.

- The High Pyrenees section starts from Zuriza in the Aragón region and continues through Catalonia to Puigcerdà. It is covered in 28 stages and 420km, taking in the most remote and beautiful parts of the mountains before reaching Puigcerdà. Puigcerdà is located in the Cerdanya plateau, an exceptionally large flat area in the mountain chain and a logic access point. Other points to access the route are Torla, Benasque, Espot and Encamp.

- The final section continues through Catalonia from Puigcerdà to the Mediterranean, and is described in 11 stages, covering 263km. It is here that the GR11 reaches its highest point (2780m) before crossing steep wooded terrain and descending to the dry and probably hot coast at Cap de Creus.

For section hikers, the whole route is divided into 5 sections, with good road access at the start and finish of

each section: these access points are Zuriza, Parzán, La Guingueta d'Àneu and Puigcerdà.

Besides these main access points, at many places the route crosses smaller mountain roads serving high villages, generally well served by bus, allowing the hiker to access or leave the route. Most routes quickly reach main bus and rail routes including the east–west rail lines between Bilbao, Pamplona, Zaragoza, Lleida and Barcelona in Spain or Hendaye, Pau, Toulouse and Perpignan in France.

The GR11 doesn't pass over many summits, but suggestions are made for climbing many of the easier peaks which could be attempted while walking the route. If you want to climb some of the more difficult, higher peaks you should ask for advice from the refuge guardians.

It would be possible to walk the GR11 from the Mediterranean to the Atlantic, but this guide describes the route from the Atlantic so that you have the prevailing wind or rain on your back and have time to acclimatise to the heat before reaching the Mediterranean.

Isard/Sarrio/Pyrenean Chamois

WEATHER AND WHEN TO GO

The Spanish south-facing slopes of the Pyrenees are much sunnier and drier than the French side and, although you can expect good weather, you should be prepared for rain and thunderstorms. The hills of the Basque Country and Navarre have a reputation for mist and spells of gentle rain, but there are also sometimes long periods of clear, hot weather here too.

The weather in the Central Pyrenees is often hot and dry, but these are high mountains and can be subject to heavy thunderstorms. Thunderstorms in high mountains are usually thought of as being an afternoon phenomenon, but in the Pyrenees the storms are often slow to build up and can arrive in the evening, or even in the middle of the night! As the Mediterranean is approached you reach an arid region and can expect hot sunny weather. Heatwaves are a common occurrence nowadays and, although temperatures are more bearable up in the high mountains, down in the valleys and near the Mediterranean Sea the heat can be intense. Snow in summer is rare, but it does occur.

The best months to walk the GR11 are July, August and September, but if you are only intending to walk the lower sections of the GR11 in the Basque Country, Navarre or Catalonia, you may prefer May, June or October, when the weather will be cooler. Occasionally there will be a year with very little snowfall, when starting the GR11 in June may be possible without running into problems in the High Pyrenees. If this is your aim, be prepared for last-minute planning, since it can still snow a lot in the month of May. Climate change has also caused autumn to set in later than it used to, so it may be possible to hike the middle sections in October. In autumn, one should in any case prepare for occasional extreme weather in the High Pyrenees.

PLANTS AND WILDLIFE

The Pyrenees are a wilderness with a wide variety of landscapes and climate zones. With such variety comes a wealth of plants and wildlife. The species mentioned below represent only a selection of those that might be seen in the region; further information can be found in guidebooks such as David Guixé and Toni Llobet's *Wildlife of the Pyrenees* (Gallocanta, 1st edition, 2016) and Christopher Grey-Wilson and Marjorie Blamey's *The Alpine Flowers of Britain and Europe* (Collins, 2nd edition, 2001).

Marmot

Mammals

The Pyrenees are home to a great number of mammals, some of which are endemic to the region. Hunting and diminishing natural habitats have at times led to the disappearance of a species, but in the last few decades great efforts have been made to protect and even reintroduce mammals in the area.

Two animals you will certainly spot are the isard and the marmot. The isard is a small, goatlike animal with vertical horns that usually lives in small herds. In the 20th century they were almost hunted to extinction, but nowadays there is a large, stable population.

When you hear the marmot's high-pitched alarm call, this usually means it has spotted you first. This small mammal, a member of the rodent family, died out in the Pyrenees because of the last ice age, but in 1948 marmots from the Alps were introduced and now there is a large population.

Another example of the reintroduction of a species is the Iberian ibex, also called the Iberian wild goat. The impressive males are much greater in size and have much longer horns than the females. The Pyrenean subspecies sadly died out in 2000, but since 2014 ibex from other regions have been released in Spain and France, resulting in the present population of around 400.

The Pyrenean bear population has a broadly similar history. The original brown bear population died out in 2004, but genetically identical animals from Slovenia and Spain have been released since 1996. There is an ongoing debate between those for and against the presence of the bear in the Pyrenees, resulting in slow progress for the species. However, the population now seems viable at around 90. Only a few bears live in the western Pyrenees; the largest group lives in the Central Pyrenees (between Parzán and Pic Carlit). The brown bear is largely a plant-eater, but it is also an opportunist, so occasionally it might attack another animal – for example, a sheep. It's extremely unlikely that a hiker will encounter a bear. Bears associate the smell of humans with danger as a result of centuries of hunting practice; a bear will run to safety as soon as its excellent sense of smell detects any human presence.

The most curious mammal in the mountain chain is the Pyrenean desman. The desman looks like a mole (and is about the same size), but has a tail like a rat's, webbed feet and a long snout which it uses as a snorkel. It lives in clean mountain streams, where it hunts for insects and sometimes small fish and frogs.

A relatively new mammal to the Pyrenees is the mouflon, a small number of which were introduced in the 20th century. A type of wild sheep, the male has impressive, curled horns. There is a chance of spotting mouflons in the eastern Pyrenees.

Clockwise from top left: Yellow-winged darter, a typical dragonfly around high-altitude lakes; swallowtail butterfly; southern white admiral; silver-washed frittilary; southern skimmer dragonfly at Cap de Creus.

Other mammals in the Pyrenees include wolf, lynx, wildcat, common genet, deer, fox, squirrel, badger, wild boar, otter and stoat.

Reptiles and amphibians

The Pyrenean rock lizard can be seen sunbathing on warm days. This small reptile has a body of about 6cm long and its tail is just under double that length. The species is endemic and occurs in a restricted area in the higher part of the Central Pyrenees, between 1600m and 3000m. In the lower parts of the entire Pyrenean range, the common wall lizard is, as its name suggests, a regular sight. This lizard has a strongly marked grey back, whereas the Pyrenean rock lizard is a more uniform grey. A much larger lizard can be seen too: the western green lizard, which has a brilliant emerald green body of up to 40cm long. Its preferred temperature is 32–33°C, so you are more likely to see it closer to the Mediterranean Sea!

When it rains, most hikers think about finding shelter, but rain is the fire salamander's favourite weather for an outing. Usually, they are active only in the evening and the night, but on a rainy day you may well spot this black and yellow creature in a forest. When they're not hunting for spiders, slugs, newts and young frogs, they prefer deciduous forests, where they like to hide in fallen leaves. The Pyrenean brook salamander is another endemic species in the Pyrenees; this largely aquatic variety

grows to 16cm long and can be seen in slow-moving streams between altitudes of 700m and 2500m.

The only venomous snake in the Pyrenees is the asp viper. This snake has a distinctive black zig-zag pattern on its back and is on average 60cm long. It likes warm areas that are exposed to the sun, with some plant cover. It occurs in the lower Pyrenees (below 2100m), notably in the limestone mountains. In the unlikely event of a bite, medical care should always be sought immediately.

Butterflies, dragonflies and damselflies

You will see butterflies occasionally, in flower-rich areas close to water. The mountain Apollo is a typical Pyrenean butterfly and other species include purple emperor, swallowtail, scarce swallowtail, southern white admiral, heath fritillary, silver-washed fritillary, Pyrenees brassy ringlet and Adonis blue.

The Aigüestortes National Park, with its many lakes, is a great place for dragonflies and damselflies; there and in other places you may find the yellow-winged darter, white-faced darter, small pincertail, golden-ringed dragonfly (which lives primarily around mountain springs), western demoiselle, common blue damselfly and large red damselfly.

Birdlife

A full list of the birds that can be seen in the Pyrenees is beyond the scope of this guide; only a small selection is mentioned here.

The Pyrenean range boasts numerous birds of prey. You will easily spot vultures, kites and common kestrels.

In terms of vultures, the Pyrenees are home to the griffon vulture, the Egyptian vulture and the bearded vulture. Vultures are of great ecological value as scavengers and these three cooperate in cleaning up the carcasses of dead animals. The griffon vulture is a very large bird with a wingspan of up to 2.5m. It can often be seen soaring above open areas, looking for food. When a carcass has been found, large numbers of griffon vultures are likely to be seen descending to the location. While they eat most of the animal, Egyptian vultures can be seen waiting patiently for their turn. Whatever the griffon vultures leave is for them. When only bones are left, the beautifully coloured bearded vulture comes into action. Its wingspan can be up to 2.8m and it is the one and only animal that specialises in feeding on bones: it lives on a diet of 90 per cent marrow. Its powerful digestive system dissolves even large bones, and those that are too large to swallow it picks up and drops onto rocks in order to break them into smaller pieces.

Kites have a wingspan of 150cm. Both the red and the slightly smaller black kites are easily recognisable by their distinctive forked tail. They are opportunistic hunters that feed on rodents, birds and small fish.

The common kestrel is a relatively small bird of prey that can often be seen hovering 10–20m above the ground, searching for prey. If prey is detected, the bird makes a short, steep dive to the ground.

Among the many other birds in the Pyrenees are two species that live along mountain streams: the yellow wagtail is a small, graceful, yellow and green bird that feeds on insects and the dipper is a small, stout, short-tailed brown and white bird that is exclusively seen on riverbanks and on stones in rivers. It is unique among small birds for its ability to dive and swim underwater. Their prey consists mainly of invertebrates and small fish.

Flowers

The Pyrenean flora is quite spectacular. There is an enormous variety of flowers and more than 160 of them are endemic – for example the Pyrenean saxifrage, a large pyramid saxifrage that decorates limestone boulders and rock faces; the Pyrenean Ramonde or Pyrenean violet, a beautiful purple flower that belongs to a large tropical family and can be found only on shady limestone rocks in early summer; and the Pyrenean thistle, a pink thistle that survives in clusters at high altitudes on scree slopes.

Common flowers that decorate the lower slopes and pastures in spring and early summer are narcissi, asphodel and gentians. In summer, mountain slopes are often filled with great yellow gentian, rosebay willowherb, alpenrose and English iris.

A good number of species of orchids are quite easily found in the Pyrenees. The black vanilla orchid is a tiny red and black orchid commonly seen in the lower moutains. In a forest you may be lucky enough to see a bird's-nest orchid blooming and in the meadows you can see fragrant orchid, burnt-tip orchid, pyramidal orchid and the beautiful lesser butterfly orchid with its white flowers.

Beside streams and in marshy areas there are globeflower, marsh marigold, common monkshood, marsh gelwort, white false helleborine and common butterwort. In forests and open spots on lower slopes there are martagon lily, Alpine sow-thistle, great masterwort or mountain sanicle, wood cranesbill, common columbine, betony-leaved rampion, spiked rampion, fringed pink, St Bruno's lily and the beautiful Pyrenean lily.

In open fields at the sub-alpine level are Alpine aster, Pyrenean eryngo, merendera, trumpet gentian, Pyrenean gentian, sweet William and the endemic spotted gentian. Where snow has just melted in summer, Alpine snowbell and Pyrenean buttercup make their appearance. Some flowers survive at high altitudes on rocks and scree: Alpine toadflax, purple saxifrage, Pyrenean thistle, Alpine hawksbeard and glacier wormwood.

Clockwise from top left: Martagon lily in the flower-rich Vall d'Estós; marsh orchid; English iris; mountain carnation.

MOUNTAIN WEATHER

Mountain ranges have a habit of creating their own climate. The weather you will experience depends a lot on the season and the hiking window you choose, but a few generalisations can be made.

First, July and August are the warmest months in the Pyrenees and below 2500m most snow will have melted by mid-July. Secondly, in the western part of the Pyrenees, rain and mist are much more likely than in the eastern part.

The Pyrenees' climate is to a great extent determined by the Atlantic Ocean. Clouds pushed in from the Atlantic start to rise against the western and northern slopes of the mountain chain, causing them to cool down and release their humidity as rain or snow. It's common to see clouds reaching up to a certain height on the northern side of the high ridge while in Spain there is blue sky. In the Basque Country there isn't such a weather frontier, so rain and mist can be persistent on both sides of the border there.

There will often be nice, warm weather in the Pyrenees, but it's important to understand that beautiful, warm weather may change to a potentially violent thunderstorm in the afternoon. It's advisable to always make an early start so you can cross high passes before this might occur. If you notice a thunderstorm approaching, try to find a safe shelter (but not a cave). If you are high up, descend

to a valley, even if that means turning back. If a thunderstorm suddenly begins and there is no safe shelter nearby, keep metal objects (such as hiking poles) at least 30 metres away and make yourself as small as possible, while minimising contact with the ground. Crouch with your feet and knees together and cover your face with your hands.

Even without thunderstorms, the heat can be extreme at times, especially close to the Mediterranean Sea. This may lead to problems like thirst, dehydration, sunburn and sunstroke. Make sure to take enough water, adjust your pace and find shelter from the heat during the warmest part of the day.

Weather forecasts are available at every staffed mountain hut and nowadays mobile phone reception is surprisingly good in many places, allowing you to check the latest forecast online. Keep in mind that it is very difficult to predict the weather for a high mountain area, so depending on your exact location you might get worse or better conditions. Be ready for anything!

GETTING THERE

Getting to the start of the trail is possible from both Spain and France. From many places it is easier to get to Hendaye in France than to Irún in Spain. Luckily it is very easy to get from Hendaye to the start of the GR11 (see Section 1). Section hikers also have several options to get onto the trail. It is again often easier to approach from the French side, but you can also get onto the trail from Spain or Andorra. For getting back home, there are good options on both sides of the Pyrenees. Useful websites are given in Appendix A.

By rail

The easiest way to get to the trailhead of the GR11 may well be by train from France. Paris can be reached by Eurostar and other trains. From here SNCF run high-speed trains (www.sncf-connect.com/en-en/tgv) to Hendaye, which is on the French–Spanish border, a short distance from Cabo de Higuer, where the GR11 departs.

For section hikers it is good to know that there are also connections from Paris to Candanchú (Col de Somport), Lourdes and Latour-de-Carol (near Puigcerdà).

By plane

Flying to Paris Charles de Gaulle airport and travelling on by train may well be the fastest option to get to the trailhead. High-speed trains to Hendaye depart from the train station located in the airport. Two other large airports nearer to the Pyrenees are in Toulouse and Perpignan.

Flying to a smaller airport close to the Pyrenees is another option, provided you find a flight there and can make your way to your preferred starting point. In France there are smaller airports in Biarritz, Pau, Lourdes and Carcassonne. In Spain too there are small airports close to the Pyrenees: you might be able to fly to San Sebastian airport (located in between Irún and Hondarribia), Pamplona or Huesca.

For getting back home from Spain, Girona or Barcelona airport can be good options. Also in Andorra there is an airport where you can fairly easily get onto one of the Andorra sections of the GR11.

By car

You could drive down to Irún through France or from Bilbao or Santander in northern Spain (which can be reached by ferry from Portsmouth or Plymouth with Brittany Ferries, for example). You will need to find somewhere to leave your car (campsites sometimes offer long-term parking) and at the end of your hike you could return to Irún by rail. The main west–east line joins Perpignan, Toulouse, Pau and Hendaye.

GETTING BACK

At the trail end, a shuttle bus departs every 30 minutes from the Cap de Creus lighthouse to Cadaqués. From Cadaqués there are frequent buses to Figueras, Girona and Barcelona. If you are travelling back from France, first take a bus from Cadaqués to the Llançà train station and travel on by train to Perpignan, where you can connect to other destinations.

If you have the time, it is worth walking back to El Port de la Selva, exploring some of the beaches on the Cap de Creus peninsula on the way, and then following part of the coastal path – the GR92 – to Llançà, or on to Portbou, where a magnificent coastal cliffwalk, starting from Portbou beach, leads you over the border to Cerbère. Once in France it is possible to follow the 'sentier litorale' (coastal path, waymarked with yellow stripes) all the way to Banyuls-sur-Mer, at the trail end of the GR10 and HRP.

WHAT TO TAKE

In terms of what to take, you should be aiming to not get cold or too warm, to have enough food and water, to be able to find your way, to keep yourself safe on the track and to have fun while hiking.

- Choice of hiking gear is very personal. Lightweight gear is recommended but it is not unheard of for trekkers to cross the Pyrenees carrying a 20kg backpack. If you make your choices based on your experience, capabilities and goals for the trip, you should be fine. Nevertheless, keep in mind that with a light pack you're likely to have more fun.

- Sending gear that you no longer need back home is sensible, and sending gear or supplies ahead to one of the post offices or campsites on the way is equally possible.

- If you are using accommodation, you may still want to carry a

Near Muskilda (Stage 6)

lightweight sleeping bag and mat which will enable you to stay in an unmanned hut or bivouac if necessary.

Essentials

- Good footwear – lightweight boots or trailrunners.
- Sock combination – wool hiking socks offer the best breathability. Use them with a liner sock to avoid blisters.
- Backpack – a capacity of around 60 litres is reasonable if you're bivouacking and carrying your own food.
- Clothing combination – a layering system gives you the greatest flexibility. Consider taking zip-off trousers, two or three short-sleeved t-shirts, a long-sleeved t-shirt in merino wool and a light insulated jacket (preferably with a hood). Carry a buff, gloves and a hat for the cold mornings and evenings.
- Waterproofs – these should be able to cope with thunderstorms in the High Pyrenees or steady rain in the Basque Country.
- Sun protection – definitely take sunglasses and a sun hat, and those who burn easily should take sun sleeves to protect their skin from the intense mountain sun.
- Drinking system – altogether, this should have a capacity of a least 3 litres. Even though you might not use it often, a water purification system can be useful.

- Wash kit – toothbrush, toothpaste, soap and lightweight towel.
- Sleeping bag liner or light sleeping bag – for use in staffed huts.
- First aid kit – a compact one for the usual cuts, sprains, blisters, stings, pains, etc. It should also include a survival blanket or bag.
- Torch – there are plenty of small, high-power torches to choose from.
- Maps and waterproof map pouch.
- Money and documents – cash, bank card, ID card and mountain club membership card.

Non-essentials

- Hiking poles – the constant climbing and descending will be a lot easier on your knees with a pair of these. In steep and rocky places, they're also a great help for your balance.
- Waterproof trousers.
- Hiking watch with altimeter.
- Camera.
- Books – a notebook for your trip report, a field guide to the Pyrenean wildlife or a novel for the evenings.
- Power bank or solar panel – gives you the freedom of charging your devices anywhere. Note that some mountain huts have limited electricity and may not allow charging; some huts ask a small sum for charging.
- Binoculars or monocular – for spotting wildlife.

Camping equipment
- Sleeping bag – a down sleeping bag with a decent comfort temperature rating is the best choice for the Pyrenees.
- Tent – a lightweight one that is able to withstand high winds.
- Sleeping mat – preferably a comfortable inflatable one. You will probably never need to pitch your tent in a place with stones, so the risk of punctures is low.
- Stove, cooking pot, fuel and lighters – carry at least two lighters and store them in different places in your pack. Note that fuel and lighters are prohibited on aeroplanes, Eurostar and some other train lines. Gas cartridges and other fuel can be bought at regular intervals, but careful planning is essential. Sale points for the different types of gas sold on or close to the trail are mentioned.

LANGUAGE AND CULTURE

Languages

Although you may think you are walking through the 'Spanish' Pyrenees, the locals won't think of themselves primarily as Spanish. You are passing through Euskadi (Basque Country), Navarre (Navarra), Aragón, Andorra and Cataluña (Catalonia).

In the Basque Country and the north of Navarre the main language is Euskera (Basque) and in Catalonia it is Catalan. These two languages are also spoken in the French Basque Country and in French Catalonia. It is less likely that you will encounter Aragonés and Aranés, but you will see the legacy of these languages in the confusion of place names. Spanish (Castilian) will be an official language in these provinces and you can expect all the locals to speak Spanish as a second language. English is now spoken much more widely, especially by younger people, and it is gradually taking over from French as a third language.

There is a lot of confusion with place names in the Pyrenees, with many different spellings. When Spain was a centralised fascist state, Spanish names were imposed on the provinces, but with the coming of democracy, the provinces have been able to show a greater degree of independence, and one expression of this is the return to place names in the local language. This means that on maps and signposts names may be given in Spanish, a local language or even in French.

Cultural identity and politics

When they were independent states, the Spanish Basque Country and Catalonia were much larger than at present and included large chunks of the Pyrenees which are now in France. Nowadays, they have a certain degree of autonomy and the independence movements in both provinces have a lot of support.

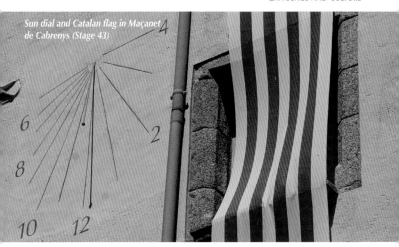

Sun dial and Catalan flag in Maçanet de Cabrenys (Stage 43)

The Spanish Civil War had a devastating effect on the people of the Pyrenees and the effects can still be seen today with the destruction or desertion of many mountain villages. The Civil War broke out in 1936 with a coup d'état by reactionary elements in the army. The position in the Pyrenees was particularly complicated as there were not only the Fascist and Republican armies, but also independence movements among the Catalans and the Basques. By the time the Republicans were defeated in 1939, about 700,000 lives had been lost and about 500,000 refugees had fled across the Pyrenees into France.

An exodus in the opposite direction occurred during World War 2, when thousands of European refugees fled Nazi-occupied territory by crossing the Pyrenees into Spain, mostly to travel on to Portugal, the UK or Belgian Congo. Often these refugees were guided over the Pyrenees by locals (so-called 'passeurs') who knew the terrain well.

The most remarkable political event in recent history was when the Catalan independence movement organised an independence referendum in 2017. The Spanish riot police used violence to prevent people from voting and independence leaders were prosecuted. Several political leaders were arrested while others fled (sometimes using small roads over the Pyrenees) into self-exile. The solidarity French Catalans showed during these events is a reminder that there is a sense of identity in the region which goes beyond belonging to a nation-state.

Andorra

Although Andorra is not in the European Union (EU), it uses the Euro. Keep in mind that when using your mobile phone in Andorra, you are out of the EU, so roaming charges will apply. Be aware that if you buy duty free products, you have not paid tax in an EU country and customs controls are in operation on road crossings to France or Spain. Catalan is the official language of Andorra, but English, French and Spanish are widely spoken. Camping laws are the same as in Spain: no daytime camping, except with the landowner's permission, but you can bivouac (with or without a tent) on uncultivated land away from habitation. Fires are not permitted.

Shops and restaurants

Remember that in many places the Spanish siesta is a lasting tradition. You can expect shops in smaller places to be open in the morning, closed during the afternoon and open again in the evening. Typically, shops may be closed from 12:00/13:00 to 16:00 or even 17:00. Supermarkets and some restaurants in towns are open all day. Other restaurants may also be closed in the afternoon, usually between 14:00 and 16:00/17:00.

ACCOMMODATION

The main Spanish holiday season is July and August. During this period all facilities will be open, but accommodation could be fully booked, especially at weekends. There is a wide range of accommodation on the GR11.

- Paradors are luxurious and expensive hotels.
- Hotels vary greatly in quality and cost.
- Hostals are basic hotels. Some will just offer accommodation, but most will also have a bar-restaurant (a hostal is not a hostel).
- Casas rurales or turisme rural are private houses offering accommodation similar to a typical bed and breakfast.
- Albergues are 'youth hostels', but they do accept adults too.
- Manned refugios or refugi are mountain huts which offer accommodation (possibly in communal dormitories). They have a drink and meals service open to both residents and non-residents, and most provide packed lunches.
- Many campgrounds will have cabins, normally called 'bungalows', and some will have bunkhouse accommodation.
- Unmanned refugios or refugi are open for the use of mountaineers and walkers. Most of these are purpose-built buildings that are well maintained by mountaineering clubs, but some are no better than unmaintained cow sheds.

The facilities described during the course of each stage description are summarised in a box at the end of each stage, in route order, with full contact details. If desperate, ask at any

Refugi de los Forestales (Stage 10)

bar-restaurant; they will often know locals who offer accommodation outside the official system.

Manned mountain refuges

Refuges vary greatly, but as a guideline you can expect the following:

- Basic accommodation for walkers and climbers.
- Refuge hours and rules are designed for walkers, not for late-night drinkers.
- You may be able to get a discount if you are a member of an Alpine Association.
- People staying in refuges usually book half board (supper, bed and breakfast) or full board (half board with the addition of a picnic bag for lunch). But it is equally possible to use the refuge only for accommodation.

- Some but not all refuges will have self-catering facilities.
- There are mattresses and blankets in the dormitories but you need to bring a sleeping bag or sleeping bag liner.
- Some refuges are open all year and others only during the summer. Many will only be open at weekends in the spring or autumn and some will open out of season if you make a reservation. At the Góriz refuge, making a reservation is essential for both staying in the refuge and for camping in the designated areas around the refuge. Only a limited number of tents are allowed. Bivouacking in the Ordesa region is forbidden.
- It is recommended that you make reservations in high summer and at weekends.

- Refuges offer a bar and snack service to walkers outside normal mealtimes.
- Refuges will normally have a separate space which can be used just like any other unstaffed refuge, but only during the time when the refuge is closed.
- Camping is not permitted in the vicinity of most manned refuges. Often it is possible to pitch a tent at a reasonable distance from the refuge.
- Many of the refuges don't have their own website, but use a regional website which operates central booking.

CAMPING

In this guide the American term 'campground' has been used for commercial campsites, to distinguish them from wilderness campsites.

In Spain car-camping used to be widespread alongside roads and dirt roads with visitors setting up camps, often for weeks at a time, in many of the most beautiful places in the mountains or around the coast. To prevent this, a general law was passed to ban wild camping, which also applied to backpackers.

The compromise, in practice, is that backpackers are allowed to bivouac for one night, with or without a small tent, well away from roads and habitation. In several national and natural parks, however, even bivouacking is forbidden.

You should ask permission if you want to camp near villages, in farmers' fields or close to a refuge. There is rarely any problem camping high in the mountains, but discretion should be used when camping at lower levels. The daily stages given in this guide are intended for those using overnight accommodation. Those who are wild camping will want to ignore these stages and camp well away from the towns, villages and refuges in their own preferred spot.

If you are accustomed to always camping beside water, you will often have difficulty in finding a suitable campsite, especially in the Basque Country and eastern Catalonia. In the High Pyrenees, campsites near water are easier to find.

Suggestions have been made in this guide as to the best campsites. These will normally be places where camping overnight is legal, and which have good grass that will take a tent peg. The experienced backpacker will find plenty of other places to camp.

It is worth camping as high as possible, where there is magnificent scenery and less chance of being disturbed. What's more, there are likely to be fewer cows, better grass and fewer mosquitos.

The three types of camping gas canisters that are commonly available are:

- The ones you pierce, referred to in this guide as 'original' canisters.

Hikers near Port de Caldes (Stage 24A)

- 'Easy-clic' resealable canisters, the main resealable system used in Southern Europe.
- Screw-on canisters, such as those manufactured by Coleman and Primus; these are the most commonly used now and in this guide have been called 'Coleman-style' gas canisters.

Where these are mentioned in the text, they were in stock when the author passed through in 2022, but – although it is likely that they will still be in stock when you pass through – it cannot be guaranteed. 'Coleman-style' canisters are becoming more readily available, but smaller places mainly use the 'original' or 'easy-clic' canisters, and these still have greater availability. Liquid fuels are most likely to be available at the ferreteria (ironmongers), but make sure you know what you are buying.

WATER

Getting enough water can be challenging if the weather is hot. You should take enough water, depending on your own needs.

Most towns, villages and hamlets in the Pyrenees have fountains with untreated spring water. The locals and most walkers will drink the water without further treatment.

You will often find fountains or 'piped' water as you walk along the trail. It should be obvious whether this water comes from a spring or a surface stream. Spring water is usually of a high quality and can be drunk with confidence. You should be more cautious about surface streams – especially woodland streams or streams in areas with sheep or cattle.

Unless otherwise indicated, the streams, springs and water points mentioned in the text were running in 2022, when there were several heatwaves and there was very little rainfall. During snow melt and during wet years there will be far more water sources, especially in the High Pyrenees.

USING THIS GUIDE

The whole route has been split into 5 sections and 47 stages. The start and finish point of each section is easily reached by public transport. Information on getting to start and finish points can be found in the section introductions. The stages have been divided with the walker who wants to use accommodation in mind. Those who are camping are advised to ignore these stages and to enjoy camping well away from towns and villages. Accommodation is limited at the endpoint of some sections so booking would be advisable in peak season. There are some sections where those requiring accommodation will have to follow the alternative route given rather than the main route.

In good visibility, when the ground is free of snow, it is possible to follow the GR11 using the waymarking, route description and 1:100,000 maps in this guidebook, but we would always recommend carrying a map, especially if you intend to follow the route in early season, when there could be extensive snowfields, or if you intend to cross high passes in bad weather (for this you should have the GPX files or detailed maps).

The publisher Editorial Alpina has an inexpensive and compact set of 21 1:50,000 maps specifically for the GR11, under the title 'Senda Pirenaica'.

Although you're unlikely to lose track of the route, navigational mistakes can occur, and they mostly happen when a walker does not look at the map or guidebook until they are lost. The route descriptions and maps in the guide are designed to prevent you from getting lost but they will be of little use when you are already lost. Keep the guidebook handy, not buried in your rucksack.

The right or left side of streams always refers to right or left in the direction of travel.

Note on the maps
The base maps used in this guide were developed from publicly available information. The contours are generally very good, and other tracks and paths are taken from open source information; they are considered to give a reasonable representation of the area and features surrounding the route.

GR11 waymarks (photo: Brian Johnson)

Water information has only been checked on the route of the GR11; streams shown on the route can be expected to run throughout the summer and the water points marked on the map are likely to be reliable through the summer, even during heatwaves.

Not all tracks and paths are marked. This is particularly noticeable at the Atlantic and Mediterranean ends of the route, where mapping the multitude of paths and tracks would have made the maps unreadable.

Timings

The timings given in this guide are estimations of the time it will take a fit hiker with a backpack to hike the stages. This does not include time for breaks or breathers, and actual walking time will depend on other factors such as navigational ability, fitness, load and conditions. Times to climb peaks assume you are walking without a pack.

Distances, climb and height profiles

Distances don't mean very much in the Pyrenees, where the steepness or roughness of the terrain can be a lot more important than the distance or the amount of climb. Distances and climb have been estimated from one specific map base. The height profiles are intended to show the general trend of the day's walk and won't show all the ups and downs.

Appendices

Appendix A lists useful contacts in the region. Appendix B provides a Spanish–English glossary. Appendix C contains a facilities table with key information about the facilities available at each stage.

GPX tracks

A GPS watch or device is not needed to follow the GR11 but can be of help when hiking in snowy conditions or in mist. GPX tracks for the routes in this guidebook are available to download free at www.cicerone.co.uk/1166/GPX. If you have not bought the book through the Cicerone website, or if you've bought the book without opening an account, please register your purchase in your Cicerone library to access GPX and updated information.

A GPS device is an excellent aid to navigation, but you should

Near Puerto de Urkiaga (Stage 3)

also carry a map and a compass and know how to use them. GPX files are provided in good faith, but in view of the profusion of formats and devices, neither the author nor the publisher accepts responsibility for their use. We provide files in a single standard GPX format that works on most devices and systems, but you may need to convert files to your preferred format using a GPX converter, such as www.gpsvisualizer.com or one of the many other apps and online converters available.

CABO DE HIGUER – ZURIZA

The Basque hills leading out of Bera (Stage 2)

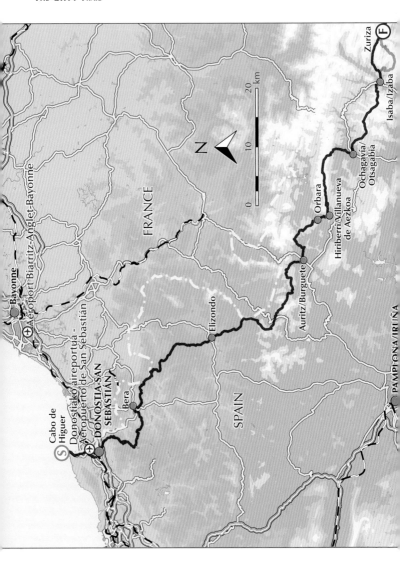

View from Ermita San Martzial to Cabo de Higuer (Stage 1)

The Atlantic Ocean and the green rolling hills of the Basque Country form the scenery at the start of the GR11. In the first week of hiking there is a gentle transition from hills and modest mountains to the first mountain over 2000m, Peña Ezkaurri. Paths are clear and easy to follow, and they very often pass through authentic, picturesque villages where you can resupply, have coffee and rest your legs for a short while, or longer. The climate is largely dictated by the close presence of the Atlantic Ocean, which means there can often be rain and periods of mist. Likewise, warm and even hot weather are possible. The landscapes are very varied, with green, rolling, bracken-covered hills,

beech forests, limestone plateaus and mountains, with their typical vegetation of rare flowers that prefer calcareous soil.

GETTING TO CABO DE HIGUER FROM HENDAYE OR IRÚN

Many hikers will arrive in Hendaye. From Hendaye train station it is 9km, or about 2hr, to get to Cabo de Higuer on foot. A logical alternative is taking the navette (a boat) connecting France and Spain. From 10:15 onwards, every 15min, the navette takes passengers from Hendaye harbour to the Benta car park in Hondarribia. It's a cheap, very short trip and tickets are bought on the boat. From Hondarribia it is a 3km (40min) walk

43

to Cabo de Higuer. Go N from the Benta car park and follow a seaside promenade named Butron Pasealekua Ibilbidea until you reach a roundabout. Turn right at the second exit and continue on Foru Kalea until the next roundabout, where you turn right at the first exit onto Ramon Ibarren Pasealekua Ibilbidea. Reach Playa de Hondarribia, the main beach of Hondarribia, at the next roundabout and continue straight onto the road along the beach. Beyond the beach, walk past the industrial harbour. A short distance after the road turns away from the ocean, turn right onto a path (signpost 'GR121') that takes you to the lighthouse, Faro de Cabo Higuer, and Camping Faro de Higuer (40m from the lighthouse).

For hikers arriving in Irún, taking the bus is a good option: route E25 will take you from the Fermin Calbéton bus stop to the Ramon Iribarren bus stop at the end of the Playa de Hondarribia (20min). From there it's a 1.6km walk to the lighthouse. Follow the route mentioned above from Playa de Hondarribia to Cabo de Higuer.

FACILITIES

- Camping Faro de Higuer has a bar-restaurant. 'Original' and 'easy-clic' camping gas for sale. Open all year. Tel 943 641 008 www.campingfarodehiguer.es
- Navette Hendaye-Hondarribia: tel 622 427 388, www.jolaski.com
- See Stage 1 for facilities in Hondarribia and Irún.

STAGE 1

Cabo de Higuer to Bera (Vera de Bidosoa)

Start	Cabo de Higuer
Finish	Bera (Vera de Bidosoa)
Time	8hr 30min
Distance	31.4km
Total ascent	830m
Total descent	820m
Difficulty	Easy. Waymarking is sparse until the southern edge of Irún, after which it is very good.
High points	Collado de Erlaitz (448m), Collado de Tellería (415m)

At the Atlantic Ocean you can dip your feet at the cliffs near the lighthouse. Once clear of Irún, the route is typical of the Basque Country as you traverse rolling hills on good tracks through a mixture of woodland and pasture. This stage is long for a first day, so if you are camping it is sensible to take three days to get to Elizondo at the end of Stage 2.

Find a large GR11 information board on the stone wall around the lighthouse garden. Go N past the sign towards the Atlantic Ocean. Follow the tarmac track, soon forking left (signpost 'GR121') along a path with GR markers which loops round the lighthouse and follows the slumping undercliff. On reaching the road, turn left down to the harbour and follow the coast road past the **Playa de Hondarribia** (**25min**), where there are water points, toilets and beach showers. There are water points at regular intervals along the seafront.

> Hondarribia is a large tourist resort with all facilities. Camping Jaizkibel, 500m west of the centre of Hondarribia, also has cabins and a bar-restaurant. Albergue Juan Sebastián Elcano is at the northern end of Hondarribia, inland from the marina. You must show the Hostelling International card in this youth hostel.

Continue past the large marina and follow Itsasargi Kalea after crossing a roundabout right by the Bidasoa river. Cross a canal and walk past the airport (**35min**). Cross another canal at the end of the airport and cross a roundabout. You are now entering **Irún**.

Irún is a large town with an international railway station. All types of camping gas are available at Decathlon in Parque Comercial Txingudi at the south-west end of Irún. There are buses to Txingudi from Hondarribia and Irún every hour.

Walk under a large road, cross a roundabout, cross a bridge over the railway and turn right onto a tarmac footpath next to a canal (**50min**). Turn left upon reaching the next bridge, then right, cross two roundabouts and continue on Alzukaitz Kalea past the second roundabout. Turn right before crossing a bridge, then continue on a tarmac footpath which eventually takes you over a small bridge and to a road. Turn right under the A-8 (Autopista del Cantábrico) (**15min**) and cross the road. There is a GR11 information board by a concrete track on your left (**10min**). The GR11 is well waymarked from here.

Turn left up the concrete track, ignoring two left forks, then continue up a rough track. Join another concrete track at Aldabe Farm, with water point, cross a road and continue up a tarmac track which becomes gravel after another house. Cross the road again and reach a large picnic area with water and toilets (190m, **35min**). Camping possible. The building on your right is the **Ermita San Martzial**, which has a bar-restaurant.

Irún, on the border of the kingdoms of Navarre, Castile and France, belonged to Navarre, but became part of Castile in 1200. In 1522 Navarre raised an army, assisted by German and French mercenaries, to recapture Irún and they defeated a Castilian army at the battle of Monte San Martzial on 30 June 1522. Success was honoured by the building of a chapel on the shoulder of the hill.

In 1813 Wellington was besieging the French garrison at San Sebastián when he had news of a relief force under General Soult. Wellington broke off

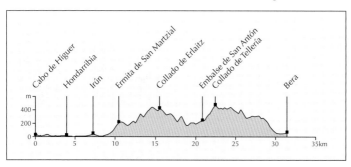

Approaching Bera through typical Navarre hills

the siege and marched his British and Spanish army to meet the French. On 31 August 1813 the Napoleonic troops were defeated in the second battle on Monte San Martzial, and the chapel became an important shrine for the people of Irún.

Continue ESE along a tarmac road, pass two playgrounds and turn right (signpost 'San Anton'). Climb up the tarmac road and soon turn left onto a dirt road. Pass a house at 1.5km from Ermita San Martzial and enter the Aiako Harria Natural Park. Follow a dirt track that becomes a small concrete road. Turn left (signpost 'Erlaitz', 340m) onto a path, pass a small white building and soon reach a picnic area right by a road (no water point here). There is a designated camping area here. Cross the car park on the Collado de Erlaitz (444m, **1hr 15min**) with **Erlaitz** (495m) on the right and **Pagogaña** (482m) on the left. It would be very easy to walk up Pagogaña from here.

Beyond the car park, continue just left of the road on a grassy track, passing through another picnic site with no water point. Continue until you reach a track going off diagonally left (392m) just after parking areas on either side of the road. The GR11 forks down the track (S). Gradually descend, forking left and veering sharp right at a junction; the rocky peak ahead is Risco de San Antón (596m). The track switchbacks down, reaching a clear-looking woodland stream at the final switchback. Continue down the track until you cross a cattle grid and come out at a small road. Turn right, uphill, to reach the western end of the Embalse de San Antón dam (Endara, 240m, **1hr 35min**). Turn left across the dam and continue along the road to pass the **Ermita de St Antón**, behind a gate on your right (**10min**). This chapel has a water point and a covered seating area.

Turn left up a concrete track signed to the Bar-restaurante Ola-Berri, just after the chapel. Before you reach the bar, the GR11 turns right over a stile and up a path across pasture, then forks left as you enter the wood and climbs steeply to reach a concrete track at the **Collado de Tellería** (Collado de San Antón, 415m, **30min**). Should the conditions be very muddy, you may prefer to stay on the concrete track left of the Bar-restaurante Ola-Berri, then switchback right and follow the track to the Collado de Tellería (415m).

Continue E along the concrete track, descending past a farm and climbing again. Keep straight on at a crossroads and fork right at some houses. Then fork right up a track, then left along the main track and left again. Turn left and right at a tiny woodland stream and then join a concrete track at a farm with a water point in the farmyard. Follow the concrete track E, fork right and then left along a path which joins a track. Soon fork right as the track becomes a path. Cross a concrete track at Alasta (357m) and follow the track along the crest of the ridge. Dry camping. Fork left after a white building at **Amargunko Lepoa** and contour to the next saddle, Amargaga Lepoa (304m, **1hr 10min**). Take the middle track, then fork left then right, then left again to start the descent to Bera. Follow the main track down to reach a minor road on the outskirts of **Bera**. Keep straight on at a crossroads before veering right to an old narrow bridge across the Río Bidasoa, which you remember from Irún.

Cross the bridge and follow the road into town, turning left along the main road to the town centre. Turn right at the Bar-restaurante Euskalduna and continue to the square, now a big car park, just after the Bera tourist office (50m, **1hr**).

Bera is a small town with a tourist office (public toilets inside), a selection of accommodation and an excellent supermarket. Ferreteria Monola stocks 'original' and 'easy-clic' camping gas.

FACILITIES ON STAGE 1 (IN ROUTE ORDER)

Camping Jaizkibel: tel 943 641 679 www.campingjaizkibel.com

Albergue Juan Sebastián Elcano: tel 943 415 164 www.gipuzkoa.eus/es/web/gazteria/equipamientos/albergues/albergue-hondarribia

Irún Tourist Office: tel 943 020 732 www.irun.org/es/turismo-ciudad

Bera Tourist Office: tel 948 631 222

Hostal Zalain: tel 948 630 967 https://zalain.info/hostal

Hotel Churrut: tel 948 625 540 www.hotelchurrut.com

Casa Rural Romano: tel 948 631 137

STAGE 2

Bera to Elizondo

Start	Bera
Finish	Elizondo
Time	8hr 20min
Distance	30.1km
Total ascent	1270m
Total descent	1120m
Difficulty	Easy. Waymarking is good.
High points	Santa Bárbara (396m), Collado Achuela (795m)

Today's walking is primarily on tracks through woodland and pasture, over steep rolling hills. This is a long day, which comes early on the GR11, but there is no obvious way to shorten it for those who are not camping.

Start at Bera tourist office. Head S from the GR11 information board along the right-hand side of the square and up a concrete track which passes to the right of a tennis court and public swimming pool before joining a tarmac road. Turn right and continue to a junction on a bend with a probably dry water point. Fork right up a track, then left and left again past a house and onto a concrete track, before forking right up a track. Rejoin the track and follow it to the final house. Take the left-hand track, still climbing, then go sharp left at a track junction onto open hillside. Fork right up the ridge to the summit of **Santa Bárbara** (396m, **1hr 5min**). On the summit you will find a concrete bunker and a collection of monuments and memorials. The high mountain to the north is La Rhune (905m) in France.

In 1939 Franco ordered the **Pyrenean border** to be fortified and militarised. The plan was to build more than 10,000 bunkers from one end of the Pyrenees to another. Initially, the reason for the fortifications was to prevent the return of the Republicans, but plans were modified to thwart a possible German invasion and finally to prevent intervention by the Allies or the Maquis (French resistance movement). Construction continued until 1952, long after there was any justification for the defences. You will see the remains of this defence line at intervals along the GR11.

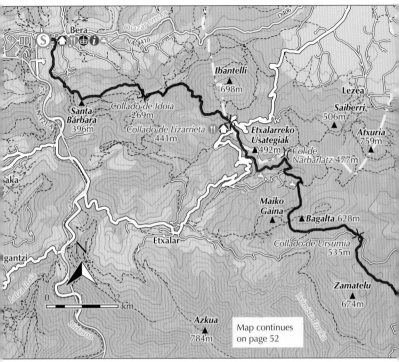

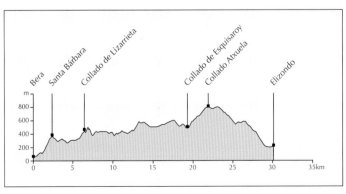

Map continues
on page 52

Veer left along the edge of the wood, descending to a saddle. Turn left, then right, then continue to a concrete road and turn right to reach the **Collado de Idoia** (269m, **25min**).

Turn left along a dirt road, forking left uphill. Higher up, fork right along a track, turn left at a junction by a delapitated barn, Dornakuko Borda, and fork right when you return to the dirt road by another barn. The road veers right as you reach the woods. Contour along the south-west slopes of Ibantelli (697m) and cross a woodland stream. Continue to **Collado de Lizarrieta** (441m, **1hr 15min**) on the French–Spanish border.

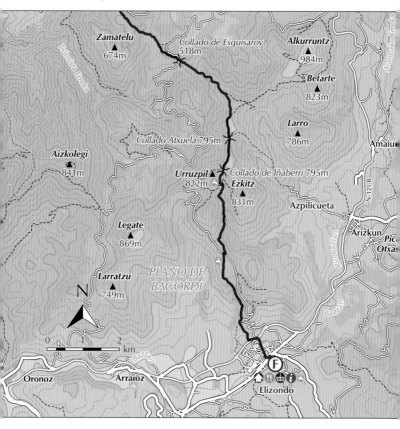

On your left, in France, is Chambre D'Hôtes Hordago Ostatua (also a bar and lunchtime restaurant) and on your right is bar-restaurant Venta de Lizaieta (open 9:00–20:00, closed on Mondays). On the French side there are also picnic tables and a seating area under a roof.

Cross the road and continue up a large track. After about 10min, at a saddle, a track joins from back right. The GR11 takes the path forking right and switch-backs down past Usategi (private hostel) before forking left and climbing past a barn with a possibly dry water point. Fork left to cross a ridge and then descend a little on the other side. The path then contours and passes another barn before reaching a junction just below the **Col de Narbarlatz** (445m, **45min**).

Fork right and follow the track downhill. Fork right and descend to a wood-land stream. Cross and veer right. Turn left up a concrete track which goes through a farmyard (370m, **5min**). Water point in the farmyard. Continue up the track, turning sharp right at a junction with a dirt road and veering left to a picnic area with a water point (440m, **25min**). Ideal camping spot.

Fork left at the picnic area. The track becomes a concrete road and veers right, after which you ignore right turns and continue straight to the top of the hill, then stay on the main track past a barn and veer left round **Bagalta** (628m). Then fork left on a grassy path to rejoin the main track. Pass a barn at the Collado de Irazako (530m) then reach a power line where there is an ancient tumulus. Stay on the main track, ignoring turns, to reach a complex road junction at the **Collado de Ursumia** (535m, **55min**). Turn right (S) along a track, following the main track at a junction, then fork right at a col to start the descent. Fork left three times during the descent, then right along a path which contours through woods before joining a track just before reaching the road at **Collado de Esquisaroy** (518m, **40min**).

Cross the road and take the path forking right. Fork right at a junction (725m, **35min**) and fork right and left as you continue to climb to a track joining from the left. Traverse right (W) of Atxuela (825m) to Collado Atxuela (795m) with a small iron cross. The track contours W of La Ronda (854m) to reach the **Collado de Iñaberri** (795m, **30min**). Excellent dry campsites.

Fork left, roughly S, ignoring a myriad of paths, then veer left into the woods and turn left down a good track and immediately right along a path which leads to Caserío de Maistuzar. Immediately after the farmhouse is a spring, Fuente de Maistuzar. The path joins a track and then forks right to reach a road at Plano de Bagordi (580m, **35min**) where there is a picnic area with a water point. Turn right and immediately left and continue S down a road which soon becomes a dirt track. Ignore a driveway on your right and several left turns and reach a white build-ing at the end of the track. Go left past the building and continue down a narrow path which takes you into a forest. Soon pass a spring, keep left at a junction and

The river Baztan in Elizondo

continue descending in the forest. Turn right just before reaching a road and arrive at a dirt road. Continue descending past a couple of farm buildings, fork left, ignore a path coming in from the right and cross a road at a few houses. Reach a track parallel to the N-121-B and turn left. Turn right soon after this track becomes a tarmac road, go under the N-121-B and walk into **Elizondo**. Cross the Río Baztan and turn left along to the main street, and after 100m reach a large church, Iglesia de Santiago (200m, **1hr 5min**), on your right. There is a water point in the churchyard.

Elizondo is a small town with a seasonal tourist office and a range of accommodation. As well as smaller shops there is a large supermarket just north-east of the church. Ferreteria Quevedo has 'original', 'easy-clic' and 'Coleman-style' camping gas.

FACILITIES ON STAGE 2

Chambre d'hôtes Hordago Ostatua: tel 0033 7 86 79 41 14 www.chambresdhotes-hordago.com

Venta de Lizaieta: tel 948 987 136

Elizondo Tourist Office: tel 948 581 517

Hotel Elizondo: tel 948 722 883 www.hostalelizondo.com

Hotel Baztan: tel 948 580 050 www.hotelbaztan.com

Hostal Antxitonea: tel 948 581 807 www.antxitonea.com

Hostal Posada Elbete: tel 948 581 519 www.posadaelbete.com

Albergue Kortarixar: tel 626 532 452 www.kortarixar.es

STAGE 3

Elizondo to Puerto de Urkiaga

Start	Elizondo
Finish	Puerto de Urkiaga
Time	5hr 20min (8hr to Albergue Sorogain in Stage 4)
Distance	17.6km
Total ascent	1090m
Total descent	395m
Difficulty	Easy. The waymarking is good but you will have to take care with navigation in mist as the route is complex and undefined in places. It will be muddy and slippery in wet conditions.
High point	Collado Bustalmorro (1170m)

This stage goes mainly through woodland and pasture on paths and tracks over steep rolling hills. The route reaches 1000m for the first time on the trail. There are no ideal campsites until you reach the Collado de Urballo.

The traditional end of Stage 3 is at the Puerto de Urkiaga, but this road pass is without accommodation, good campsites or water! The main option for those requiring accommodation would be to continue to Albergue Sorogain, which is just over 2hr ahead (see Stage 4). An alternative would be to use Hostal Arrobi Borda whose owners offer transport to and from the Puerto de Urkiaga.

Head up Calle Mauricio Berecoechea, immediately right (W) of the church. A left and right turn lead you out of town to reach a GR11 information board (216m). Fork right up a track, then soon fork right again and take the middle path before rejoining the road. Follow the road for about 100m then turn right along a path which veers left. Turn left at a track and immediately right. Turn right when the track continues through a gate, then fork left up a path, passing to the right of a farm. Join a track and turn right along a path (361m, **45min**) as you come close to the road.

Continue climbing, cross a concrete track (**15min**) and pass a spring (435m). When the track switchbacks right, veer left along a path and pass another spring. Higher up cross a stream and keep straight on, steadily climbing until you reach

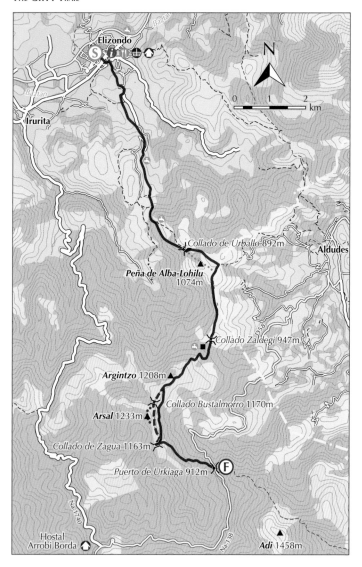

a track (470m, **40min**). Turn right, then fork left at a switchback on a major track. Keep straight on along a grass track when the major track bends left, soon passing a water point (10m left of the track) with good campsites. The track narrows to a path and climbs gradually to arrive at a hunter's cabin (888m, **40min**) just below the **Collado de Urballo**.

> The hunters' cabin has a water point (open a tap underneath a metal lid to make the water run) and picnic tables.

Continue up to the col; camping is possible here. In good visibility you could easily climb Peña de Alba-Lohilu (1074m) to the SE. Continue straight (W) up a small path, soon forking right. The paths are a bit nebulous with many sheep tracks, so follow the waymarks carefully as you contour the grassy northern flank of **Peña de Alba-Lohilu** and reach the border fence at Border Stone 127.

> In 1659 the **Treaty of the Pyrenees** was signed on an island in the Río Bidasoa to end the 1635–1659 war between France and Spain, and a new border was fixed at the Pyrenees. However, the border was not properly settled until the Treaty of Limits in 1856. Border Stone 127 is one of about 600 numbered stones that were positioned in the 1860s to designate the border.

Pass ancient tumuli as you follow the fence along the ridge. Eventually, after a couple of shooting towers, leave the border fence as it veers off left. Soon reach another fence, which also veers off left before you reach an earthen track. Fork right just before a gate to reach a hunting cabin with a water point and benches

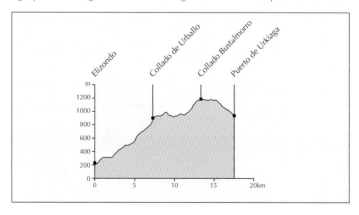

Early morning at Collado Zaldegi

at **Collado Zaldegi** (947m, **1hr 15min**); camping is possible here. There are better dry campsites on the ridge ahead.

Veer right up the track, and right again to the right of two more hunters' cabins to pick up a path heading NW, before swinging SW. Climb out of the woods and steeply up to a col below **Argintzo** (1208m). Cross the fence at a stile (1139m, **35min**) and veer right, to the left of the fence. Follow waymarks along faint animal tracks round the south-eastern flank of Argintzo to rejoin the ridge and fence at a saddle (1158m, **15min**). The GR11 now contours on the eastern slopes below **Collado Bustalmorro** and Arsal, but in good weather you may prefer to follow the ridge over Arsal (1233m) before reaching broad, grassy **Collado de Zagua** with signpost (1163m, **25min**).

The GR12 continues along the ridge, but turn left on the GR11, veering right of a white cabin. Pass a cabin where you pick up a track, which is followed, ignoring all side turns, to the NA-138 road at **Puerto de Urkiaga** (912m, **30min**). This minor road connects Aldudes in France to Zubiri in Spain. There is little traffic on this cross-border road so it could be difficult to hitch the 20km down (S) to Zubiri, on the Camino de Santiago, where there is accommodation. While it would be possible to camp here, there aren't any good sites. In an emergency you could use one of the old wartime concrete bunkers on the route ahead.

Hostal Arrobi Borda, which is just up the NA-1740, about 6km down the NA-138, has accommodation and a bar-restaurant, and offers free lifts to and from the GR11 from the Puerto de Urkiaga for those staying at the hostal.

FACILITIES ON STAGE 3

Hostal Arrobi Borda: tel 948 304 709 www.arrobiborda.com

Hosteria de Zubiri: tel 948 304 329 www.hosteriadezubiri.com

STAGE 4

Puerto de Urkiaga to Burguete (Auritz)

Start	Puerto de Urkiaga
Finish	Burguete (Auritz)
Time	5hr 10min
Distance	17.2km
Total ascent	765m
Total descent	780m
Difficulty	Easy. You are following small paths for much of the section and will need to keep a close eye on the waymarking.
High points	Collado Aratun (1212m), Menditxipi (1213m)

The route crosses two grassy ridges before descending a wooded river valley. If you have any excess energy, a visit to Roncesvalles would be worthwhile. From this stage on you can expect to see griffon vultures and red kites regularly.

Head up the concrete track and soon turn left up a route through the woods which takes a shortcut back to the track. After 1km there is a large, modern bunker on the left of the path, which could make a good emergency shelter. Continue up the concrete track, which becomes a dirt track as the gradient eases. Fork left (**35min**) and then fork right as the track splits into two poor tracks. At about 1175m, fork left along a path to reach a gate at **Adipeko Lepoa** (**15min**). Good,

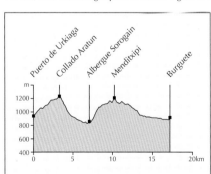

dry campsites. Turn right along small paths which start just above the wood opposite. Contour on grassland along the north slopes of Adi (1458m, large cromlech site on your left), passing a small seasonal spring, before picking up a track through the woods to reach a grassy saddle, **Collado Aratun** (1212m, **20min**). Good, dry campsites.

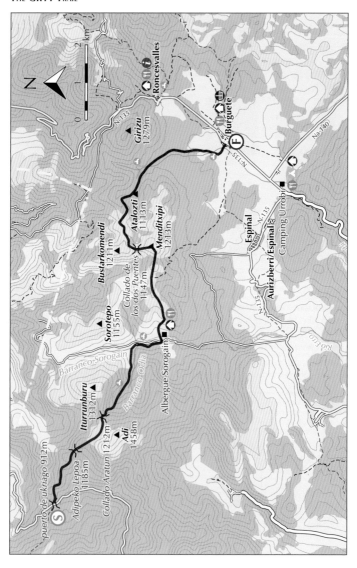

Near Menditxipi 1213m

Veer right to a stile over a fence and drop down steeply. Take care not to lose the waymarked route and eventually reach the confluence of two clear-looking woodland streams (at about 940m). Continue left of the Barranco Odia, crossing it by a bridge (895m) and crossing it again (865m), possibly getting wet feet. There are now good campsites (cows permitting) as you follow the stream down to the minor road in the Sorogain Valley. You may prefer to follow the road S from here, but the waymarked route veers right, recrosses the Barranco Sorogain and follows its right-hand bank. Cross the stream, possibly now dried up, as you approach the **Albergue Sorogain** (845m, accommodation and bar-restaurant, **1hr 10min**).

Head roughly E from just north of the Albergue Sorogain and climb past the remains of a small wind turbine. Keep a close eye on the waymarks as you are following nebulous sheep tracks which head up the grassy hill. Eventually reach a fence which is followed to a track (1069m). Continue up grassland beside the fence to the top of the hill (1181m, **1hr 15min**). Cross the fence and follow it E to a saddle (1141m) and up the other side, turning left along a fence at the top to the summit of **Menditxipi** (1213m, **15min**).

Continue N, crossing a fence to pick up a track just before the **Collado de los dos Puentes** (1147m). Veer right along the track to Uztarketako Lepoa (1112m). Continue along the grassy track to a minor top, Atalozti (1113m, **20min**). The GR12 goes straight on from here but the GR11 turns right (ESE) down a grassy ridge, passing a sculpture, to enter the woods. Descend on a track through the woods and cross a woodland stream which you follow downstream. There are good campsites alongside the stream. Continue to a gate where you join a tarmac track (898m, **50min**). This is followed until you reach the church of **Burguete** (898m, **10min**).

> Burguete is an authentic village with good facilities for tourists to cater for Camino de Santiago walkers. Turn left up the road for Hostal Burguete and, at the top of the village, a well-stocked supermarket beside a picnic area with water and toilets. Turn right down the road for the bakery, bank, Hostal Juandeaburre and Hotel Loizu, which offers discounts to hikers. There are also several casas rurales offering accommodation in the village. Camping Urrobi, which is about 2km south-west of Burguete, has a 42-bed hostel and cabins as well as camping facilities and a small shop with 'original' camping gas.

There is also plenty of accommodation and a tourist office at Roncesvalles, about 3km north of Burguete. Roncesvalles is an important monastery on the Camino de Santiago, and is the starting point for many pilgrims on the journey to Santiago de Compostella.

FACILITIES ON STAGE 4

Albergue Sorogain: tel 948 392 148 www.alberguedesorogain.com

Hotel Loizu: tel 948 760 008 www.loizu.com

Hostal Burguete: tel 948 760 005 www.hotelburguete.com

Hostal Juandeaburre: tel 948 760 078

Camping Urrobi: tel 948 760 200 www.campingurrobi.com

Roncesvalles: www.roncesvalles.es

STAGE 5
Burguete to Hiriberri (Villanueva de Aezkoa)

Start	Burguete
Finish	Hiriberri (Villanueva de Aezkoa)
Time	4hr 45min
Distance	17.4km
Total ascent	695m
Total descent	670m
Difficulty	Generally easy walking. The trail allows for fast hiking until the descent to Orbara, which is steep and will be slippery when wet. The route is complex, but the waymarking is good.
High point	Ridge below Latxaga (1185m)

This is a walk over easy wooded hills followed by a steep descent to Orbara. You get your first view of the limestone cliffs which are the major feature of the hills over the next few days.

Misty forest on the way to Nabala

Leave the village to the left of the church to reach a GR11 information board. Head ESE along a tarmac track, turn left immediately after crossing the stream and pass a picnic site. At a junction, go straight on into woods through a green gate and up a rough track, heading roughly E – ignoring all turns – to a gate at the top of the wood (1035m, **45min**). Pass through the gate then turn sharp left, heading roughly NW back into the wood. Fork left and cross another gate at 1005m. Soon reach a saddle (1015m) and turn left. Join another rough track to a saddle with signpost, **Nabala** (1013m, **30min**). Follow a good farm track and ignore turns as it contours the south slopes of Ortzanzurieta

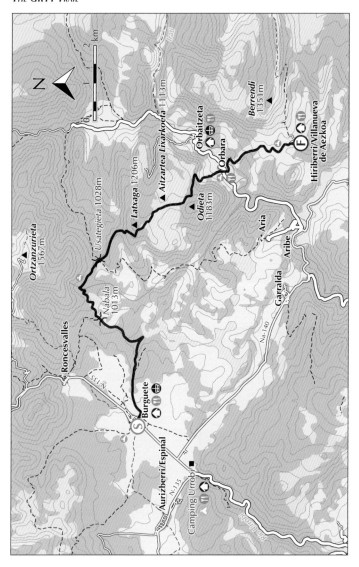

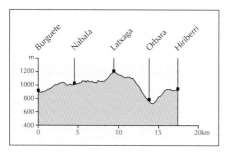

(1567m). Cross a woodland stream (**15min**) at a cattle grid and follow the good track to a major junction at another saddle, **Usategieta** (1028m). Cross the cattle grid and turn right up a track climbing roughly SE through the forest. GRT-8 goes off left at Txutxurieta (1048m, **30min**) while the GR11 keeps straight on along a path. When you reach a fence with a stile, climb over and switchback up the hill, veering right well below the top and crossing some pasture to another fence.

Cross the fence, go sharp left and continue climbing to the wooded summit ridge (1185m, **30min**) of Latxaga (1206m). Keep straight on, soon veering right to an open ridge. Superb, sheltered, dry campsites. It isn't long before you re-enter the forest and follow the waymarks until you eventually reach a good track. Turn right along it, through farmland, and cross a tarmac road at Aitzartea Lixarkoeta (1113m, **20min**).

Keep straight on, cross a stile and soon re-enter the woods. A little later, at a signpost, you pick up an old path which winds its way downhill, finding a route through the vertical limestone cliffs above Orbara. The limestone on the path will be slippery when wet. A short section of track completes the descent to the church at **Orbara** (767m, **55min**). Turn right at the church passing the bar-restaurant and water point.

> Orbara is a nice, quiet village with a bar-restaurant, Eskola Taberna. Most of the houses were modernised or rebuilt during Spain's building boom.
>
> Orbaizeta, about 30min walk (3km) along the road to the north-east, is a village with a range of facilities for tourists, including Albergue Mendilatz.

Turn right along the main road, then turn sharp left and down a concrete track. Fork left down to a bridge over the Río Irati. Cross the river and fork right up a path, which takes you up the hill. When you reach a dirt road near the top of the hill, turn right along it to a saddle with a large barn at a road junction, Aldeartea (927m, **50min**). Keep straight on along the tarmac road into **Hiriberri**, passing a water point, and up a cobbled street just to the right of the church of Hiriberri (923m, **10min**).

Hiriberri is a very authentic, charming hamlet. It has a bar-restaurant, Bar Berrendi, a hostal/bar-restaurant, Hostal Alaitze, and several casas rurales (two of which are listed below).

FACILITIES ON STAGE 5

Orbaizeta: www.orbaizeta.com

Albergue Mendilatz: tel 948 766 088 www.mendilatz.com

Hostal Alaitze: tel 948 764 393

Bar Berrendi: tel 948 764 031

Casa Rural Aguerre: tel 627 749 221 (mobile) www.aguerre.es

Casas Txikirrin: tel 948 764 074 www.txikirrin.com

STAGE 6
Hiriberri to Ochagavía (Otsagabia)

Start	Hiriberri
Finish	Ochagavía (Otsagabia)
Time	6hr 50min
Distance	20.6km
Total ascent	820m
Total descent	970m
Difficulty	The first 2hr of this day are in rough limestone 'karst' terrain, after which it is easy walking along high grassy ridges. The route is complex and although the waymarking is generally good, there are some places where a compass will come in handy, especially in bad weather. The limestone will be slippery when wet.
High points	Abodi Occidental Idorrokia (1492m), Muskilda (1071m)

The limestone cliffs of Berrendi (1351m) dominate Hiriberri. There is some rough terrain as the GR11 finds a way up through the cliffs and continues along a wooded ridge covered with limestone pavement. After this it is easy walking along the high exposed grassy ridges of the Sierra de Abodi, with sinkholes and limestone pavement to add interest. Camping above Hiriberri will have to be shared with cows and horses, but this won't be feasible until you are clear of the limestone karst.

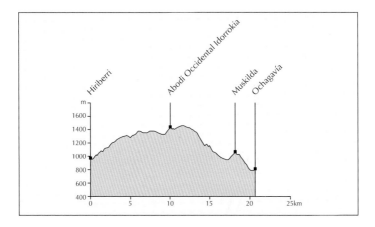

Turn left at the church, go up a cobbled street and then up a concrete track to a GR11 information board at the edge of the hamlet. Head up a stony path and veer right through a gate. Follow the waymarks up stony pasture to a large concrete cattle trough where there is good water from a pipe (**20min**). Continue to the right of the trough, taking care to follow the waymarks, going up a wide path. This path takes you past another water point (**45min**). You soon fork left up a faint path into the woods (1145m, **30min**). This path switchbacks left and follows a slightly better path up the hill to find a gap in the crags lining the escarpment. On reaching the ridge, cross a fence and turn right (1275m, **20min**). A faint path leads up Berrendi (1351m) to the west.

Follow faint paths up the wooded ridge of Sierra de Abodi. This path is very rough and rocky in places. You get occasional views of the cliffs before reaching a high point of about 1375m and starting the descent. Camping is not possible on this rocky ridge. Eventually descend slightly and cross a fence into easier, rough pasture (**50min**), passing left of a cattle pen on the ridge, and follow the track E. There are excellent but exposed dry campsites all along the ridge. You soon fork right off the track at a small, fenced reservoir and follow a grassy track along the ridge.

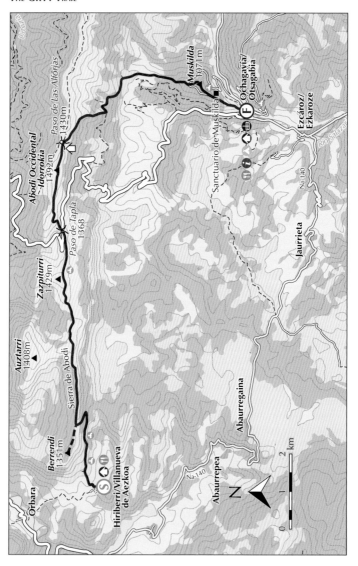

Shortly after crossing a fence the track becomes a good track, which is followed past **Zazpiturri** (1429m) to reach a GR11 signpost. Just left of this sign you should be able to obtain good water where it flows into a cattle trough (1374m, **50min**).

Continue to the **Paso de Tapla** (1368m, **10min**), where you cross a road at its highest point. Keep straight on up the grassy ridge, picking up a rough track which switchbacks to the top of the ridge (1460m). From here you could climb Idorrokia (1492m), the western top of Adobi Occidental Idorrokia to the north. Continue E along the grassy ridge to the main summit of **Abodi Occidental Idorrokia** (1492m, **45min**). Keep straight on to the **Paso de Las Alforjas** (1436m, **15min**) where there are several limestone sinkholes.

The GRT-10 and GR12 continue along the ridge, but the GR11 goes off diagonally right. You will notice a small concrete hut (this can be used only as an emergency shelter) on your right. Descend the well-marked route, keeping above the valley on your right, before descending directly down the hill to cross a fence and go down a grassy ridge to a track at the top of the forest. Turn left along the track. Good camping with the possibility of water from a stream below. Soon reach a sharp right-hand bend and then, at a left-hand bend, fork right down a faint path that leads to an old path which will be slippery when wet. Eventually rejoin the track (1039m, **1hr**). Turn right and pass a barn. Last good dry camping before Ochagavía.

Continue along the grassy ridge past a shallow saddle (Urrua Xubri, 1000m) to another farm building to reach a GR11 signpost as you enter the wood (985m, **15min**). The GR11 continues along the main track, climbing gently through the woods. Go straight across the tarmac road which provides road access to Muskilda and follow the track, which becomes a good path by the time it takes you over the summit of **Muskilda** (1071m) and down to the Sanctuario de Muskilda (1014m, **25min**) with a water point and picnic site.

Ochagavía

The shrine of **Our Lady of Muskilda** is a 12th-century Romanesque chapel that was restored in the 17th century. Inside the church is the 15th-century carved wooden image of Our Lady of Muskilda. There is a festival and pilgrimage on 8 September each year to honour the patron saint of Ochagavía.

Isolated places, such as Muskilda, were once the meeting places of covens of wizards and witches. There is evidence that the Salazarese coven met here in 1540. Salazarese is the valley occupied by Ochagavía, and the mayor of the valley was one of the participants.

The GR11 leaves the picnic area on the right to reach the far side of the sanctuary and then follows an old, cobbled path – slippery when wet – all the way to the cobbled streets of **Ochagavía**.

The GR11 comes out at the church in Ochagavía, where you continue down – roughly S – to reach a bridge over the Río Anduña (770m, **25min**). The tourist office, the Fuente de Liria, some small shops and a shady seating area are upstream to the left.

Ochagavía is a large village with plenty of facilities for tourists, including a tourist office, a hotel and hostal, several casas rurales, a supermarket and several other shops. Camping Osate at the southern end of the village also has cabins, hostel accommodation, a bar-restaurant and a shop.

FACILITIES ON STAGE 6

Ochagavía Tourist Office: tel 948 890 641

Hotel Rural Auñamendi: tel 948 890 189 www.hotelruralaunamendi.com

Hostal Orialde: tel 948 890 270 www.hostalorialde.es

Camping Osate: tel 948 890 184 www.campingosate.net

STAGE 7
Ochagavía to Isaba (Izaba)

Start	Ochagavía
Finish	Isaba (Izaba)
Time	5hr 20min
Distance	19.1km
Total ascent	675m
Total descent	635m
Difficulty	An easy day ending in a steep descent.
High point	Collado de Saitsederra (1363m)

Most of the day is spent walking on good tracks through woods and along high grassy ridges before a final steep descent down woodland paths. There are plenty of dry campsites but no water on this stage.

Cross the narrow pedestrian bridge over the river, turn right and then soon left to reach a GR11 information board. Climb steeply on a narrow path, cross a road and continue climbing steeply. The path becomes a track as you continue climbing. Fork left onto a small path, reach a dirt road at 1010m and turn left. Follow the dirt road as it climbs steadily through forest and farmland until a track joins from back right (1210m, **1hr 50min**). Keep straight on, forking left 15min later and eventually passing **Borda de Arrese** (**40min**), a concrete hut which makes a good overnight shelter, at the head of the valley. Keep going to a major junction with a signpost at Zotrapea (1309m, **20min**). Keep straight on along the middle of the three tracks ahead, soon forking right up a grassy path which rejoins the track at a shallow saddle. From here follow the track as it contours right of **Alto de la Sierra** (1415m). Ignore a major track which drops down to the right as you start contouring the north

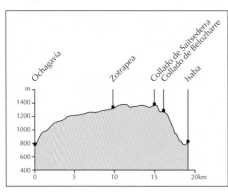

71

The hills are slowly making way for 'real' mountains

slopes of Kakueta to arrive at the **Collado de Saitsederra** (1363m, **1hr**) where the track veers sharp right. From here you could climb the grassy north-east ridge of Kakueta (1583m).

> There is a good view ahead of the **'whaleback' ridge** of Peña Ezkaurri (2047m), which will be the objective tomorrow.

The GR11 leaves the track and continues slightly right along a grassy ridge, veering further right then left to join a rough track which leads to the **Collado de Belozharre** (1358m, **20min**). Turn right here, steeply down an earthen track into the woods and continue down to a signpost (1259m, **10min**). Turn sharp left along a path which contours around the head of a valley before resuming the well-waymarked descent. Fork right at a junction (1126m, **20min**) and right again at a path junction (905m) to arrive at Idoia Dona Marialtea (Sanctuario de Nuestra Senora de Idoia) (879m, **25min**). This 16th-century chapel contains a 13th-century Gothic carving of the Virgin of Idoia.

Pass through a gate into the garden of the chapel, which has a water point and shady seating; this would be a good place for a break before arriving in Isaba. An old, cobbled path lined with crosses leads from the garden and passes a reliable water point, Fuente San Pedro, before reaching the road on the outskirts of **Isaba**. Turn left, passing Hotel Isaba, to reach the centre of the village (800m, **15min**), where there is a shaded seating area next to a small park and children's play area. There is a water point just down Calle Barrikata from here.

Isaba is a village with a tourist office and a good range of accommodation (some listed below). There are two supermarkets up the main road from the seating area. The larger is the best for food, but the smaller store also stocks a selection of other goods for hikers, including 'original' and 'easy-clic' camping gas.

FACILITIES ON STAGE 7

Hostal Ezkaurre: tel 607 395 773

Hostal Onki Xin: tel 948 893 320 www.onkixin.com

Hostal Lola: tel 948 893 012 www.hostal-lola.com

Albergue Oxanea: tel 948 893 153 www.albergueoxanea.com

Pension Txiki: tel 948 893 118 www.pensiontxiki.com

There are also a number of casas rurales.

STAGE 8
Isaba to Zuriza (GR11)

Start	Isaba
Finish	Zuriza
Time	2hr 50min
Distance	10.8km
Total ascent	595m
Total descent	180m
Difficulty	This route is easy and low level.
High point	Collau d'Arguibiela (1295m)

The GR11 follows a short and easy trail to Zuriza. However, the best scenery is found on the GR11.4 (see Stage 8a) which leaves the hills of Navarre behind and enters the first 'real' mountains. If the weather is stable and you have the time, it is worth following the GR11.4 over Peña Ezkaurri. In bad weather it is wise to follow this GR11 stage instead.

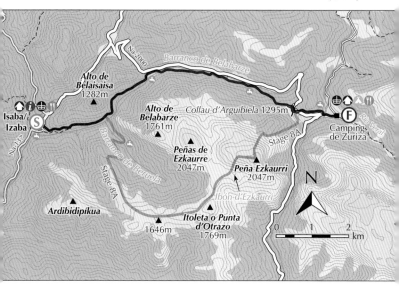

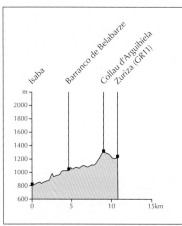

There is a 30km annual race, the **Camille Extreme**, held at the end of June, starting and finishing at Isaba. It follows the approximate route of the GR11 to Zuriza before following the GR11.4 in reverse over Peña Ezkaurri and back to Isaba.

From the seating area on the main road, fork right down Calle Barrikata, passing the water point. Keep straight on down this street to the GR11 information board on the edge of the village. Continue along the path, past a shrine, the Ermita de Belén (Hermitage of Bethlehem), and reach a dirt road. Turn left and climb to a road junction below the towering cliffs of the Ateas de Belabarze and **Alto de Belaisaisa** (883m, **35min**).

Fork left and follow the track, which leads to a place where you have the Isaba-Zuzira road (NA-2000) on your left and **Barranco de Belabarze** on your right. Ignore a dirt road which turns S to go over the barranco and continue W towards the road for a short distance. Turn right just before reaching the road (**30min**) and walk S on a path. Cross Barranco de Belabarze, climb a little, and then turn sharply left into the forest. There is good camping with water close by 15min ahead. Cross a few side streams, after which you gradually turn NE away from the river (**55min**) and climb. Reach Collau d'Arguibiela at a tarmac road (here you cross from Navarre into Aragón, 1295m, **30min**). Cross the road and continue on a path. The GR11.4

View to Peña Ezkaurri from the low-level route

soon comes in from your right. Follow a path for about 1km before descending to the road. Turn left and pass a swimming hole under the bridge before arriving at **Camping de Zuriza** (1210m, **20min**). The entrance to this large campground is on its north-eastern side.

The holiday complex at Zuriza is open all year. It includes a campground, hotel, bunkhouse, cabins, a bar-restaurant and a supermarket (only open July and August) which sells 'original' camping gas. The water point is at the far end of the buildings. At the time of writing the campsite was being restructured, so it would be wise to check the latest developments if you plan on staying there.

FACILITIES ON STAGE 8

Camping de Zuriza: tel 974 370 196 www.campingzuriza.org

STAGE 8A

Isaba to Zuriza via Peña Ezkaurri (GR11.4)

Start	Isaba
Finish	Zuriza
Time	7hr
Distance	16.7km
Total ascent	1390m
Total descent	970m
Difficulty	The GR11.4 route involves scrambling up and down broken crags on a steep limestone peak. Although the scrambling is easy, it could be intimidating for the inexperienced walker with a heavy rucksack. Waymarking is adequate on the wooded lower slopes and is good higher up the mountain. In wet weather the limestone will be very slippery, and it would be sensible to follow the official route rather than this recommended variation. In a high-snow year there may be significant snowfields on the ascent in June.
High point	Peña Ezkaurri (2047m)
Note	For map see Stage 8.

From the seating area on the main road, fork right down Calle Barrikata, passing the water point. Keep straight on down this street to the GR11 information board on the edge of the village. Continue along the path, past a shrine – the Ermita de Belén (Hermitage of Bethlehem) – and reach a dirt road. Turn left and climb to a road junction below the towering cliffs of the **Ateas de Belabarze** and **Alto de Belaisaisa** (883m, **35min**).

The official route of the GR11 continues straight on, but our featured route (GR11.4) turns right across the **Barranco de Belabarze**. The water is difficult to reach here. Continue to the roadhead (943m, **25min**). Go right, down a rough track to cross the **Barranco de Beruela**. This stream is likely to be running well, but cows use this area so you may prefer to treat the water. Head up a possibly boggy, earthen track, switchbacking once until a small, muddy path – which is easy to miss – goes off left (**10min**). Turn sharp left up this path, which climbs below a fence. When the fence turns right (**10min**) uphill, so does the path. Continue up this small path. The waymarking and path quality improve as the path veers left across pasture (**25min**). This is the first good, dry campsite. Continue climbing and eventually reach an open area on the ridge with a ruined stone hut (1295m, **20min**).

The gradient now eases as you head up the ridge, through a final section of forest, to reach the grassy ridge (1395m, **20min**). Follow the markers up the ridge, not the more prominent animal tracks which tend to contour the slopes. Veer left of **Peak 1646** to arrive back on the ridge at a shallow saddle (1600m, **45min**). Exposed, dry camping is possible anywhere along the ridge. Follow the ridge to another

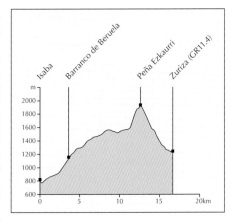

shallow saddle, then veer left, contouring the north-west slopes of **Itoleta o Punta d'Otrazo** (1769m); it would be easy to climb this peak from here.

Continue to a saddle (1654m) with a few trees and an electric fence. The GR11 markers first loop left of the fence, then cross and loop right, then they cross again and loop left to return to the fence just west of the Ibón d'Ezkaurri. This shallow lake could be no more than a polluted pond or even completely dry. Go diagonally right to find a waymark at the foot of the limestone wall of Peña Ezkaurri (1655m, **1hr 5min**), just north of the western side of the pond. The waymarked route up the face is mainly steep, rough walking, but there are a few rock steps to climb. The gradient eases before you reach the summit ridge (**55min**). There are some fairly sheltered, grassy dry campsites on the plateau. Veer right up the ridge. The waymarked route passes about 50m to the left of the summit of **Peña Ezkaurri**, which is marked by a trig point and countless cairns (2047m, **15min**).

Return to the waymarked route and follow it roughly NNW down a well-marked path, before veering right (NE) between limestone slabs to arrive at the top of the wood (1694m, **35min**) just above Collau d'Abizondo. This descent will be very slippery in the wet. The path continues down to the saddle then turns right, descending steeply through the woods to a road. Turn left to a sign on the brow of the hill at the Collau d'Arguibiela (here you cross from Navarre into Aragón, 1295m, **40min**). The GR11 joins from the left here. Turn sharp right, following a path for about 1km before descending to the road. Turn left and pass a swimming hole under the bridge before arriving at **Camping de Zuriza** (1210m, **20min**). The entrance to this large campground is on its north-east side. Practical information on the camping is found under the GR11 route description.

ZURIZA – PARZÁN

Climbing to Circo d'Esper (Stage 11)

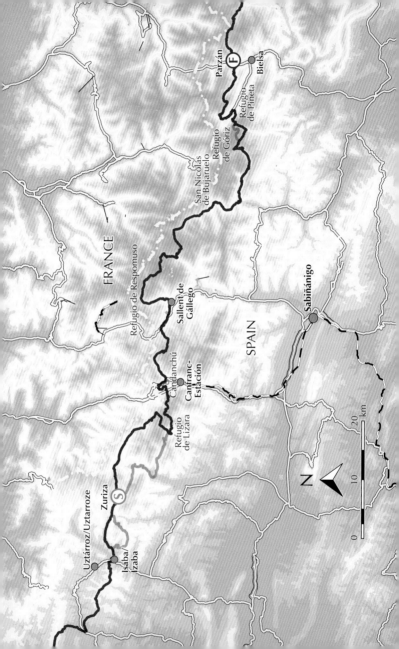

FRANCE

SPAIN

Parzán

(F)

Bielsa

Refugio de Pineta

Refugio de Goriz

San Nicolás de Bujaruelo

Refugio de Respomuso

Sabiñánigo

Sallent de Gállego

Candanchú

Canfranc-Estación

Refugio de Lizara

Zuriza

(S)

Uztárroz/Uztarroze

Isaba/Izaba

N

0   10   20

km

Folds in Circo d'Esper (Stage 11)

High mountains, challenging mountain passes and impressive scenery are awaiting you in the second section. In Stage 11, the Circo d'Esper gives a first taste of the High Pyrenees. During the first half of this section you still pass villages every day, while towards the end you will stay in the mountains before going down to Parzán. You will pass a variety of impressive landscapes as you walk the second section of the GR11. The high mountains around Respomuso include the Balaïtous, the first 3000er in the Western Pyrenees. Next are several challenging mountain passes, offering amazing views. The GR11 then takes you through the deep Ordesa canyon, a unique glacial valley shouldered by very impressive walls. In the same area you find yourself in Europe's highest limestone massif, where many hikers' main aim is to scale Monte Perdido (3355m). The GR11 contours the highest mountains of this massif, visiting the Añisclo and Pineta valleys on the way, and hikers can enjoy splendid views to the beautiful eastern side of Monte Perdido before descending to Parzán.

STAGE 9
Zuriza to La Mina (GR11)

Start	Zuriza
Finish	La Mina
Time	4hr 10min
Distance	11.5km
Total ascent	840m
Total descent	820m
Difficulty	A straightforward stage over good paths with beautiful views of the surrounding mountains.
High point	Cuello Petraficha (1964m)

You are now entering mountainous terrain. The limestone cliffs of the Sierra d'Alano are a magnificent sight. You can now expect to find water at regular intervals and wild camping is usually no problem. As you enter the high mountains, GR waymarking is often supplemented by cairns. At the end of the stage there is a good unstaffed refuge.

Head SE along the dirt road from the campsite. Notice Fuente Fría on your left after 15min, with water welling up from underground. Fork left (signpost) just before the road crosses Barranco Taxera (1289m, **35min**) and hike up the eroded path to Refugio de Taxera (1426m, **25min**), now a ruin. If you want to camp soon or need water, contour until you reach the **Barranco Petraficha** where there are plenty of campsites close to water, then head upstream to rejoin the GR11. The GR11 climbs diagonally left from the refugio and continues to

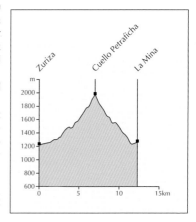

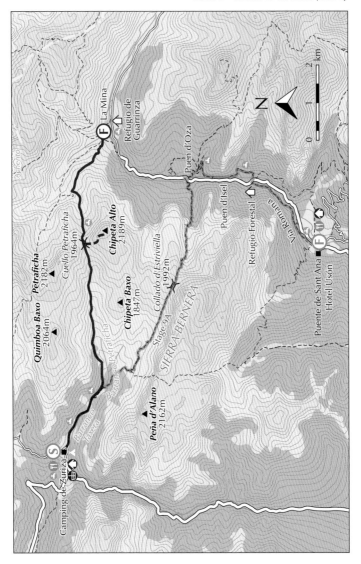

View down to La Mina

climb through the forest. Fork right as the path levels, cross a stream and descend slightly to regain the Barranco Petraficha. Follow a faint well-waymarked path up the left-hand bank of the stream. Care will be needed to follow the path in mist.

You may well hear and possibly see your first **marmot** of the trip up this valley. You may also see your first sarrio.

Pass left of a small doorless metal shed in a grassy bowl, which goes under the grand name of the Refugio de Chipeta Alto and is for emergency use only. Good dry campsites. Continue E up a rocky ridge in the centre of the valley to reach the **Cuello Petraficha** (1964m, **2hr 5min**).

It is worth climbing **Chipeta Alto** (2189m) to the south-east from here. Climb the path to the south before veering left up easy grass slopes to the ridge then along the grassy ridge to the summit, which is a magnificent viewpoint. The summit of Chipeta Alto is an impressive rocky prow with vertical crags on its north-east and south-east faces (30min up, 15min down).

Don't get confused by a path contouring left, and follow the waymarks down the valley ahead. There is water from a spring after 15min. After returning to limestone terrain you reach a path junction (1545m, **25min**). Turn right on a grassy shoulder and follow the path as it descends past the Refugio Sabucar. This refugio is more of a barn, which is well used by animals and has holes in the roof. Descend the grassy slope SE. The official route follows a faint switchbacking path, but it's easier to head straight down the slope to reach a bridge with an old GR11 information board at **La Mina** (1230m, **40min**).

If you are not camping, continue E past the parking and turn right onto a path which takes you to a bridge over Río Aragón Subordán. Continue E on the other side and soon reach Refugio de Guarrinza, a wooden shelter which sleeps eight and is being maintained by a local trail angel (eight places, **10min**).

STAGE 9A
Zuriza to Puente de Santa Ana (GR11.1)

Start	Zuriza
Finish	Puente de Santa Ana
Time	6hr 15min
Distance	18.3km
Total ascent	1050m
Total descent	1340m
Difficulty	This GR11.1 variant is well-waymarked and without difficulty.
High point	Cuello d'Estribiella (1992m)
Note	Near the end of this stage there is accommodation: Hotel Usón is right at the end of this stage, and also early on Stage 10a there is camping close by and a staffed refugio 2.5km into the route. For map see Stage 9.

This route follows the GR11.1 to Puente de Santa Ana. The GR11.1 is also followed in the following stage, 10A, which leads you to Refugio de Lizara.

Head SE along the dirt road from the campsite until you reach Barranco Taxera (**35min**). Cross the river and follow the path SE, signed Achar de Alano, which shortcuts the switchbacks in the track until you are just above two barns (**50min**). The GR11.1 follows the winding track ESE. At 1560m the track gradually becomes a path, which climbs to the **Collado d'Estriviella** (1992m, **1hr 30min**) and descends to **Puen d'Oza** (1150m, **1hr 15min**) with a picnic site and youth camp.

Cross the bridge and follow the GR65.3.3 signed 'Camino Viejo Puente Sil'. This was the old main route (Via Romana) up the valley before the road was blasted out of the cliff face. Climb, ignoring some left turns, to cross the Barranco Esparta before returning to the road at **Puen d'Ysil**. Again, don't cross the bridge

View to Sierra d'Alano (photo: Brian Johnson)

but continue along the GR65.3.3 on the western bank to cross Barranco del Jardin and return to the river. Cross the bridge and road (**1hr 10min**). There is a basic unmanned hut (**Refugio Forestal**) here.

Take the path signed 'Via Romana' and climb to the extensive remains of Lo Castiello Biello before descending easily down a good path. After crossing a stream turn left at a junction, heading down to the road. Cross the road and soon reach **Puente de Santa Ana** (920m, **55min**).

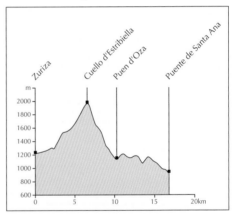

FACILITIES ON STAGE 9A

Hotel Usón is 300m to the south on the road you crossed near the bridge: tel 974 375 358 www.hoteluson.com

At the start of Stage 10a there is also accommodation:

Camping Borda Bisaltico (camping, bungalows, hostel, bar-restaurant): tel 974 34 89 40 bordabisaltico@hotmail.com

Refugio Gabardito: tel 974 37 53 87 info@refugiogabardito.com

STAGE 10

La Mina to Refugio de Lizara (GR11)

Start	La Mina
Finish	Refugio de Lizara
Time	6hr 45min
Distance	20.2km
Total ascent	1170m
Total descent	860m
Difficulty	There is good waymarking throughout the route. The north-facing slopes above Ibón de Estanés can hold snow well into summer on a high-snow year.
High points	Col north of Punta Alta d'a Portaza (1909m), Puerto de Bernera (2115m)

An easy climb up a typical alpine valley is followed by a high-level hidden valley. On the ascent up the valley there are lots of cows, making it unfit for camping. Staying at the unstaffed refuge about a third of the way into the route is a better choice. Beyond the refuge, the route now climbs to the impressive Valle de los Sarrios before crossing the Puerto de Bernera (where there is another shelter). Further down on the descent to Refugio de Lizara there is also a small unmanned shelter.

Go E past car parking and follow a track along the north side of the valley. The waymarking is absent at the start but begins to appear when you pass Refugio de la Mina on your left and the track becomes a path (despite the promising name, this military building is not open to the public). Continue ESE and pass a mound with several ancient burial chambers (**35min**). Water is available from many small side streams. Continue until a bridge is crossed (**1hr 5min**) and then climb more steeply up the right-hand side of the stream. Cross (**35min**) and recross a track before reaching the unmanned Refugio de Aguas Tuertas (small but cosy, four places, emergency phone) at **Achar d'Aguas Tuertas**, where the car track coming from La Mina ends (1615m, **15min**).

In the Stone Age, inhabitants of these mountains would have been hunter-gatherers, living in caves. As the climate improved and the domestication of sheep, goats, cows and dogs occurred, they became nomadic livestock

Candanchú

Puerto de Somport 1631m

Road tunnel

Cuello Causiat

Puerto d'Estanés 1810m

Gave d'Aspe

Cirque d'Aspe

Punta Gabedallo 2245m

Puerto de Bernera 2115m

Pico Royo 2176m

Achar d'Aguas Tuertas 1615m

Aguas Tuertas

1909m

Refugio de Ordelca

SIERRA BERNERA

Punta Alta d'a Portaza 2421m

Barranco d'a Rueda

Bisaurin 2670m

Refugio de los Forestales

Castiello d'Acher 2384m

Secus 2351m

Collado de lo Foratón 2016m

Refugio de Lizara

Río Arga Subordán

Puntal Alto de lo Foratón 2154m

Puntal d'Agüerri 2447m

Stage 10A

Refugio Plan d'Aniz

SIERRA DE CABAS

La Miña

La Cuta 2149m

Refugio de Gabardito

Refugio Dios Te Salbe

La Cuta Baxa 2062m

Hotel Usón

Borda Bisaltico

N

0   1   2 km

farmers. In the Iron Age, probably influenced by the influx of people from Central Europe, agricultural settlements started to develop in the mountain valleys. In the meadows, just north of the hut, is one of the best-preserved prehistoric **dolmens** in the Pyrenees. A burial chamber is protected by slabs of rock weighing several tonnes and would have been covered by a tumulus (a large pile of rocks and earth). Dolmens were built from the Neolithic Age until well into the Bronze Age (3000–1500BC). During this period the inhabitants of the Pyrenees buried their dead deep within caves or within dolmens. You will also find cromlechs in these mountains, dating from about 800–300BC. These circles of stone would have contained the ashes of cremated corpses.

From the refuge, contour along a path through fallen boulders to the right of the marshy water meadows of the Aguas Tuertas. The path edges down onto the flat floor of the valley and follows the path through it until you cross the Barranco d'a Rueda (1615m, **35min**), possibly getting wet feet. Excellent camp-sites. Follow the well-waymarked path, gradually veering E, then fork right at a junction marked by a post (**10min**) and climb to an unnamed col (1909m, **55min**) north of Punta Alta d'a Portaza.

Follow waymarks down a complex route which twists and turns to reach a small stream and continue to a junction where La Senda de Camille descends to Ibón de Estanés (1840m, **30min**). Keep straight on to reach a flat area, then veer right and climb to reach the lip of the hidden valley, Valle de los Sarrios (2010m, **25min**).

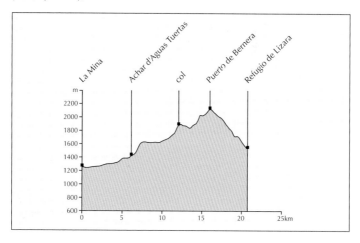

Arriving at Refugio de los Forestales

Walk along the flat, possibly marshy, valley floor and then veer right to the broad col, **Puerto de Bernera** (2115m, **25min**). Continue down into another hidden valley, Valle de Bernera, and exit on the left, crossing the valley's outlet stream (**20min**). Soon pass the Refugio de los Forestales (1967m, eight places, basic, fireplace, good views). Continue down, often high above the stream, and veer right to descend past the **Refugio de Ordelca** (1700m, four places, basic, **40min**). Continue down to a signed junction and turn left along the track to reach the **Refugio de Lizara**, a modern refuge with full refuge facilities (1540m, open all year, 75 places, **15min**).

FACILITIES ON STAGE 10

Refugio de Lizara: tel 974 348 433 www.refugiodelizara.com

STAGE 10A

Puente de Santa Ana to Refugio de Lizara (GR11.1)

Start	Puente de Santa Ana
Finish	Refugio de Lizara
Time	4hr 45min
Distance	12km
Total ascent	1175m
Total descent	555m
Difficulty	This second part of the GR11.1 is well waymarked and without difficulty.
High point	Cuello de lo Foratón (2016m)
Note	For map see Stage 10.

Stage 10A brings hikers who wanted staffed accommodation at the end of Stage 9A back to the GR11. Again, the stage follows the GR11.1 but, more importantly, it follows 'La Senda de Camille', a circuit of six huts in the Parque Natural de los Valles Occidentales in Spain and the Parc National des Pyrénées in France. This route is waymarked in green/yellow, as well as with GR waymarks. You will be walking through spectacular mountain scenery, which provides an excellent alternative to the main route. Look out for the very rare lammergeier, also known as the bearded vulture, which can often be seen on the route.

Cross the Puente de Santa Ana, turn right and continue along the road until a path goes left up the hill (**15min**) signed 'Gabardito'. Continue along the road if you want to get to Camping Borda Bisaltico, otherwise turn left up the path which shortcuts the road. There is a water point, Fuente de Baladin, at the first road crossing, then you cross the road five more times before reaching **Refugio de Gabardito** (1363m, **1hr 15min**).

Take the track roughly E from the refuge, ignoring three left forks. The track soon becomes a good path as it climbs through spectacular limestone cliffs. Fork right at a sign (**40min**) and climb to emerge above the cliffs into rolling grassland. Good campsites here and ahead. The streams on the plateau may dry up in a hot summer and in this cow country the water will need treating before drinking. Cross a small stream and pass a small hut, **Refugio Dios Te Salbe** (1550m, **30min**).

Refugio de Lizara in sight

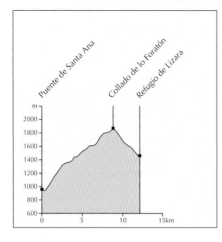

You soon pass **Refugio Plan d'Aniz**, a herdsman's hut, which is above the path on the left. Cross a larger stream and continue to reach a broad col before a rising traverse takes you to **Collado de lo Foratón** (2016m, **1hr 15min**).

From here you could climb **Puntal Alto de lo Foratón** (2154m) to the south-west (20min up, 15min down). Bisaurin (2670m) to the north is also a relatively easy climb from the col. Another option is to climb La Cuta (2149m) from Refugio Dios Te Salbe, then traverse the Sierra de Gabás before descending to rejoin the route at the Collado de lo Foratón.

The descent starts ENE before switchbacking down and passing a possible water point. Reach a track and follow it past another water point, Fuente de Fuenfría, to reach a junction with a path left signed to Ibón d'Estanés, where you rejoin the GR11. Continue down to the **Refugio de Lizara** (1540m, **50min**).

Refugio de Lizara is a modern, manned refuge with full refuge facilities.

FACILITIES ON STAGE 10A

Camping Borda Bisaltico (camping, bungalows, hostel, bar-restaurant): tel 974 34 89 40 bordabisaltico@hotmail.com

Refugio Gabardito: tel 974 37 53 87 info@refugiogabardito.com

Refugio de Lizara: tel 974 348 433 www.refugiodelizara.com

STAGE 11
Refugio de Lizara to Candanchú

Start	Refugio de Lizara
Finish	Candanchú
Time	5hr 55min
Distance	14.8km
Total ascent	1060m
Total descent	1030m
Difficulty	There is excellent waymarking throughout the route. In a high-snow year you may have to cross snow on the way to Puerto de Aisa.
High points	Puerto de Aisa (2262m), Paso de Tuca Blanca (2207m)

Unless you've already been up Peña Ezkaurri in Stage 8A, this is your first high-level traverse. There are magnificent views of the sheer limestone cliffs of the Sierra de Aisa.

Head NE from the refuge along a grassy track through the Plano de Lizara. The track starts climbing to reach a sign just before a shepherd's hut (566m, **20min**). Fork left up a faint path and climb to the left of the Barranco del Articuso. Follow the path all the way to the **Collado del Bozo** (1995m, **1hr 20min**). Ignore the right turn onto the GR11.1 and traverse left, signed Collado de Esper, and enter a hanging valley trending NNE. Head up left of the stream, following it as it veers to the right. Follow the waymarks carefully through a limestone maze as the GR11 climbs gently to the right-hand side of the wide **Puerto de Aisa** (also named Collado de Esper, 2262m, **1hr 10min**). Cow-free water point just below the col.

The descent down the steep slopes is easy at first and then requires you to cross boulders at Circo d'Esper. A few chains help you over the steepest parts. There is scree and boulderfield before you reach one of the feeder streams of the Gave d'Aspe (2020m, **35min**). Now continue on a rising traverse of the north ridge of Pico de Aspe to arrive at **Paso de Tuca Blanca**, with the top station of a chair lift (2207m, **1hr**). Switchback down the ski piste beneath the chair lift to reach a small col, Puerto de Tortiellas (1973m, **20min**).

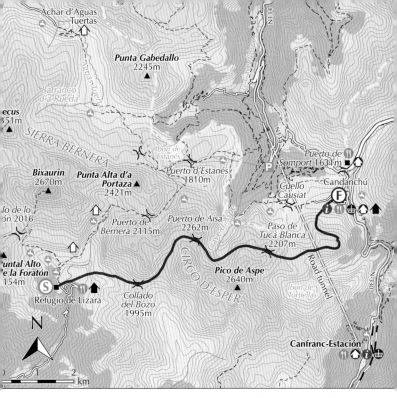

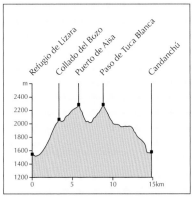

Keep straight on, climbing slightly to pick up a major track beyond more ski-lifts. Contour the south face of Peak 2049, passing a rough shelter. Keep contouring as you pass a vehicle shed and eventually cross the ridge (1963m, **25min**). The track now switchbacks down. Eventually (**25min**) fork right on a grassy path and soon turn right, following the line of ski-tows to reach the main car park above **Candanchú** (**10min**). Turn right and soon pass

95

French hiker on the way to Candanchú

Refugio Pepe Garcés and the supermarket, then head downhill past a water point and information office before turning sharp right to reach Refugio-Albergues Valle de Aragón and El Aguila (1570m, **10min**).

Candanchú is a ski resort with plenty of facilities for tourists, most of which are closed in summer! You should find several bar-restaurants open, but the supermarket is only open in the high summer. The supermarket and Deportes Galindo, a sports shop, sell 'Coleman-style' gas cartridges.

Hotels Edelweiss and Candanchú are open throughout the summer and others will be open in high summer. Refugio-Albergues Valle de Aragón and El Aguila are only open in July and August; however, they will also open for you if you make a reservation in April, May, June and September. Albergue Aysa, at the Puerto de Somport, has accommodation, a bar-restaurant and minimal supplies and is open all year.

Full tourist facilities will be open in Canfranc Estación about 5km to the south. This international railway station (at the time of writing it is being renovated) is a tourist resort with a good choice of hotels, hostals and casas rurales. There is also a supermarket.

In France SNCF run a bus service from the Puerto de Somport to Bedous to connect with the French rail network.

In Spain Mavaragon run a bus service from Puerto de Somport via Candanchú to Canfranc Estación and on to the much larger Jaca.

FACILITIES ON STAGE 11

Albergue Aysa: tel 974 373 023 www.albergueaysa.com

Candanchú Tourist Office: tel 974 373 194

Refugio Pepe Garcés: tel 974 372 378 www.refugiopepegarces.com

Albergue Valle del Aragón: tel 974 373 222 reservas@candanchu.com

Refugio-Albergue El Aguila: tel 665 198 833
www.alberguelaguila.com

Hotel Edelweiss: tel 974 373 200 www.edelweisscandanchu.com

Hotel Candanchú: tel 974 373 025 www.hotelcandanchu.com

Canfranc Tourist Office: tel 974 373 141 www.canfranc.es

STAGE 12
Candanchú to Sallent de Gállego

Start	Candanchú
Finish	Sallent de Gállego
Time	6hr 40min
Distance	23.9km
Total ascent	905m
Total descent	1180m
Difficulty	Mostly easy hiking. There is a steep climb to Ibón d'Anayet.
High point	Ibón d'Anayet (2227m)

The GR11 goes via the Canal Roya and the Ibons d'Anayet, where there are magnificent views to the Pic du Midi d'Ossau (2884m), just over the border in France. Punta d'as Negras (2441m) and Pico d'Anayet (2574m) dominate the views at the start of this stage.

From the Albergues Valle del Aragón and El Aguila continue downhill for 600m and, when the road turns sharply to the right, leave the road by turning left onto a path. Cross the N-330a road (**10min**), which joins Spain to France over the Puerto de Somport, and continue on a tarmac road. The GR11 coincides with the GR65-3, a variation of the Camino de Santiago. Soon fork right and continue on a path. Turn left and follow a track by a large white building. Pass the Anglassé Chimney.

> The **Anglassé Chimney** is the last surviving relic of the mining industry (silver, copper and iron), and dates back to the 16th century. There was also a factory for making combs, knives and buttons and an inn for use by cross-border travellers.

Continue to a well-signed junction (1375m, **40min**). You could turn right if you need to resupply in Canfranc. On the right side of the road you find a short driveway to the **área recreativa de Canal Roya**, with a small, basic bothy, running water and excellent places to pitch a tent. The GR11 continues left along the track and passes the Fuente del Cerezo (1460m, **15min**). Water. Fork right at a sign and cross the Río de Canal Roya on a bridge and continue along the right bank.

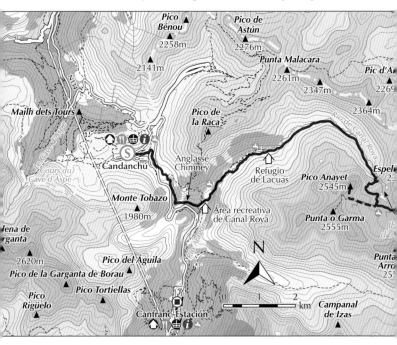

Pass **Refugio de Lacuas** (1550m, **30min**), a small shelter which could be of use in an emergency. Continue, often high above the stream, gradually veering SE

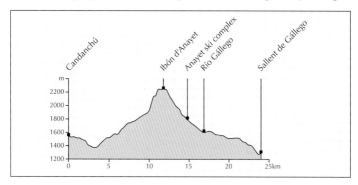

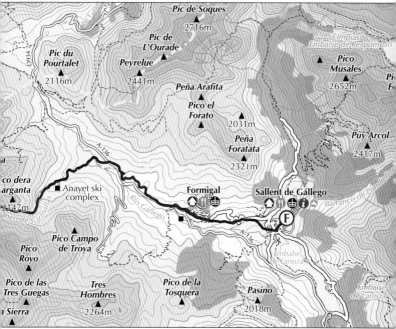

The iconic Pic du Midi d'Ossau seen from the lower Ibon d'Anayet

into the Plano d'a Rinconada and reach the lip of a flat grassy area with a dolmen in the middle of it (1865m, **1hr 15min**). Good camping.

It seems as if you are reaching a dead end with the intimidating climb up to Ibones de Anayet in front of you, but in reality this climb goes over good paths at all times. Follow the path up the right-hand side of the small cirque heading for the lowest crags. The path is well cairned with occasional waymarks. The path crosses a stream and then switchbacks easily through the crags to emerge at the top (2225m, **1hr 10min**). Now head E and you arrive at the **Ibón d'Anayet**. Good campsites. There is a second smaller lake below to the north, which is better for swimming. The impressive mountain to the north, in France, is the Pic du Midi d'Ossau, probably the most photographed mountain in the Pyrenees.

It would be possible to climb **Anayet** (2574m) by its south-western ridge from the Cuello d'Anayet (2413m). An easier peak is Punta Espelunciecha (2399m) to the east of the lakes, which can be climbed by its southern ridge (30min up, 15min down).

The GR11 skirts the right-hand edge of the meadow to the south of the Ibón de Anayet and over grassy moraine to reach the top of the descent. This could be confusing in mist as there are old paths and waymarks, but if in doubt keep close to the left bank of Barranco Anayet. Further down, the path crosses the stream several times before arriving at the **Anayet ski complex** (1747m, **1hr 5min**).

Walk down the ski road, which is closed to traffic in summer, and pass to a gate at the end of the road to reach the A-136 road at a car park (1550m, **25min**). Cross the A-136 and turn right onto a path at a signpost. It isn't always easy to

On the way down to Formigal with the brown-white Picos del Infierno easily recognisible in the background

find the waymarks in the vegetation, especially when the route turns sharply left to navigate around a wet area, but in general you stay at a short distance of the A-136. Reach the A-136 again just before Formigal, turn left and follow the road. Fork left at the first roundabout, enter **Formigal** and continue straight on at the second roundabout. Turn right after 500m, at the east end of Formigal, just beyond a small building on your right. Go down a path and reach a track. Turn left and follow the track E, cross a road several times and walk into Sallent de Gállego. Turn left as you reach Calle Puente Romano and walk on with Río Aguas Limpias on your right side. Reach the main square of **Sallent de Gállego** where there are bars, restaurants, shops and a water point (1295m, **1hr 10min**).

Sallent de Gállego is a small town with plenty of hotels, a selection of bar-restaurants and shops. Gorgol Mountain stocks 'Coleman-style' camping gas and Petruso Outdoor Store sells 'Coleman-style' and 'original' camping gas.

FACILITIES ON STAGE 12

Sallent de Gállego Tourist Office: tel 974 488 012

Hotel Balaitús: tel 974 488 059 www.hotelbalaitus.com

Hotel Bocalé: tel 974 488 555 www.hotelbocale.com

Hostal Centro: tel 974 488 019

Gorgol Free Mountain: www.gorgol.com

STAGE 13

Sallent de Gállego to Refugio de Respomuso

Start	Sallent de Gállego
Finish	Refugio de Respomuso
Time	3hr 55min
Distance	11.1km
Total ascent	955m
Total descent	30m
Difficulty	Easy
High point	Refugio de Respomuso (2220m)

This is only a short day, but it leaves you in position to climb the Collado de Tebarray and Collado del Infierno in the morning on the following day, which is safer, since you would not want to be caught on these high passes in an afternoon thunderstorm. On the other hand, if you are here early in the season when there is still snow on the climb to Collado de Tebarray (enquire at the refugio), it is wise to start at around 10:00–11:00 to allow the snow to become soft. You are entering a region of granite mountains which provides some of the most spectacular scenery in the Pyrenees.

Leave the main square on the left (north-east corner) and head out of town on streets just left of the stream, then follow a signed path along the riverbank to a bridge. Continue up the track on the left bank of the stream. Turn left at a well-signed junction and follow an old walled path up to a road (**35min**). Turn right, forking left just before the dam (1438m, **10min**). Follow the path along the south-western shore of the **Embalse de la Sarra** to arrive at the northern end of the reservoir (1438m, **15min**).

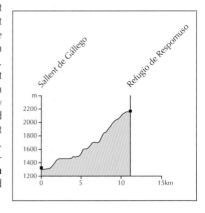

On your right, on the other side of Río Aguas Limpias, is Bar-restaurante Asador la Sarra, with a picnic area, covered outdoor shelter, water point and car park. Continue up the excellent path past the Plana Tornadizas, a recreational area with picnic table. Good camping spots. Further on you won't find many camping opportunities until after the Refugio de Respomuso.

Now climb up a wooded gorge, often high above the Río Agua Limpias. Ignore a path left signed to Collado la Soba shortly before the gorge narrows at the Paso de l'Onso (1700m, **1hr**). The path follows a ledge along the cliff face. The

Crossing a barranco on the way to Ibón de Respomuso

path veers E, passing another left turn signed to Ibones de Arriel (**20min**), which you ignore, and you climb a long V-shaped valley through a granite landscape. Fork left as you approach the dam to reach a signpost (2160m, **1hr 20min**) just north-west of the Ibón de Respomuso.

The GR11 goes straight on for a short distance before forking left and switch-backing up the slope, then contouring well above the northern bank of the reservoir and forking right to the **Refugio de Respomuso** (2220m, **15min**). There is no camping by the refuge, but there are plenty of good campsites above the eastern shore of the reservoir and up to the Ibón de Llena Cantal.

The Refugio de Respomuso is a large, modern manned refuge with normal refuge facilities. It is open all year and can be very busy at weekends in the summer as it is the base for the popular climb of Balaïtous (3144m) to the north.

FACILITIES ON STAGE 13
Bar-restaurant Asador La Sarra: tel 974 563 480
Refugio de Respomuso: tel 974 337 556 www.alberguesyrefugios.com

STAGE 14

Refugio de Respomuso to Baños de Panticosa

Start	Refugio de Respomuso
Finish	Baños de Panticosa
Time	6hr 20min (considerably longer in snow)
Distance	12.4km
Total ascent	715m
Total descent	1300m
Difficulty	This is the most difficult stage on the GR11, with an ascent up a very steep gully to the Collado de Tebarray and steep descents from here and from the Collado del Infierno. There is a lot of boulderfield to cross and there will be snow on the route in early season and possibly well into the summer. It is advisable to get over the pass in the morning as it would be dangerous to be caught in an afternoon thunderstorm while crossing the passes. If there is snow on the way to Collado de Tebarray (enquire at the refugio) it is wise to start at around 10:00–11:00 to allow the snow to become soft.
High points	Collado de Tebarray (Piedrafita) (2765m), Collado del Infierno (2721m)
Note	If you don't need the facilities at Baños de Panticosa you can take the unofficial GR11 variant starting at Refugio de Bachimaña.

The route passes through superb alpine scenery. The Collado de Tebarray is the most demanding col on the GR11. This is not a route for the inexperienced in poor weather or in early season when a steep snow slope will need to be climbed.

Follow waymarks SE from the Refugio de Respomuso past the old refuge which is now locked. Continue roughly SE past the eastern tip of the reservoir. Turn left and, close to the stream draining the Llena Cantal valley, turn right along a faint waymarked path (2140m, **40min**). The path crosses the stream twice before veering away from it to reach Ibón de Llena Cantal (2438m, **1hr**). The campsites on the eastern shore of this lake are the last comfortable sites until the Ibón Azul Alto.

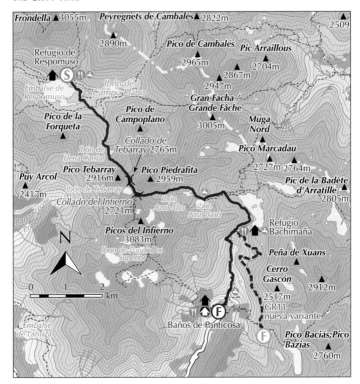

The path follows the western shore of the lake before veering left up a rocky ridge and following a stable path up the moraine. You appear to be heading for a dead end below the cliffs, but you veer right up an uncomfortably steep gully partially equipped with a chain. Take care not to dislodge stones on to those below. Arrive at a rocky notch in the ridge, **Collado de Tebarray** (2765m, **1hr 20min**). The rocky east ridge of Pico Tebarray (2893m) allows for a relatively easy climb to the top.

A steep but short descent on the other side leads to a path contouring left across the moraine above the Ibón de Tebarray to the **Collado del Infierno** (2721m, **15min**). There is a popular climb of the three Picos del Infierno (3073m–3082m–3076m) from here – be warned that it involves some exposed scrambling and requires excellent route-finding skills.

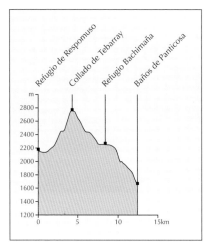

Descend the well-way-marked route. The route crosses the stream twice before passing left of the **Ibón Azul Alto** (**30min**). This lake has the first good campsites on the descent. Climb a little before descending to the dam of the **Ibón Azul Baxo** (2360m, **15min**). The waymarked path crosses the outlet stream and recrosses to descend to the left of the stream. It could be easier to stay left of the stream. Reach a flat grassy area (**25min**) with a signpost just above the large Ibón de Bachimaña Alto. Turn right across the stream and follow the path which traverses up and down high above the western bank of the reservoir to reach the dam of the Ibón Baxo de Bachimaña (**25min**). From here it is 200m to the **Refugio de Bachimaña** (2200m).

Refugio Bachimaña is a large, modern manned refuge offering a full refuge service. It is open all year.

Ibón de Tebarray

Refugio Bachimaña at Ibón Baxo de Bachimaña

Shortcut avoiding Baños de Panticosa

If you don't need any facilities at Baños de Panticosa then you can follow an unofficial GR11 variant route which connects Refugio de Bachimaña and a junction with the GR11 at 2200m on Stage 15. It is a high-level route which keeps above 2100m but also involves some descent and ascent. It is shorter and faster compared to the GR11, but not by much (1hr 40min vs 3hr 25min; 4.2km vs 6.3km). The ascent/descent is 360/325 vs 580/560. The main reward is that you stay in a high mountain landscape and avoid going to the busy and touristy Baños de Panticosa. The route is not marked with GR markers, but it is cairned and has red dots in a few places.

Depart SE from the Refugio Bachimaña, go in between rocks and reach a path at Río Caldarés. Turn right, and almost immediately fork left and cross Río Caldarés. Fork left after 150m and continue climbing. At 2250m ignore a path that turns left to Ibón de Coanga and descend. Continue descending when the path turns sharply right and soon cross a bridge over Barranco de Lavaza (2185m, **30min**). Continue descending W to 2100m (**50min**), where the route turns sharply SSE and forks left at a junction. This junction is easily missed, so make sure you don't start going down to Baños de Panticosa here! Climb up and continue SSE, following a pipeline (passing through two small tunnels) and ignoring the path to Ibones de Serrato. Finally rejoin the GR11 at 2205m (**1hr 45min**). You are now on Stage 15 at a junction of paths where you should follow the GR11 W towards the largest Ibón dero Brazato.

Main route from Refugio de Bachimaña to Baños de Panticosa

From the refuge return to the dam and follow the well-marked path down the right-hand side of the Río Caldarés, which flows down a beautiful granite valley.

You pass a flat, grassy area beside the stream. The last camping before Baños de Panticosa is here. Ignore bridges to the left as you continue down the right-hand side of the stream to reach the Refugio Casa de Piedra on the edge of Baños de Panticosa (1635m, **1hr 30min**). The water point is outside the Hotel Continental.

Baños de Panticosa is a spa resort catering for those with big budgets. It has a lot of parking, which attracts a lot of day hikers, as well as hikers doing a multi-day circuit in the area.

Fortunately there is a refuge, Refugio Casa de Piedra, which has a full refuge service and is open all year, as well as the 5-star Gran Hotel (with casino) and the 4-star Hotel Continental. There is also a café, bar and restaurant, but only a souvenir shop.

FACILITIES ON STAGE 14

Refugio Bachimaña: tel 697 126 967

Refugio Casa de Piedra: tel 974 487 571

Booking for Refugio Bachimaña and Refugio Casa de Piedra:
www.alberguesyrefugios.com

Central reservations for Gran and Continental Hotels: tel 974 487 161
www.panticosa.com

STAGE 15

Baños de Panticosa to San Nicolás de Bujaruelo

Start	Baños de Panticosa
Finish	San Nicolás de Bujaruelo
Time	7hr 15min
Distance	19.9km
Total ascent	930m
Total descent	1225m
Difficulty	There are long sections of boulderfield on this stage. The crossing of the Río Ara could be difficult in snowmelt or in wet weather.
High point	Collada Alta de Brazato (2566m)

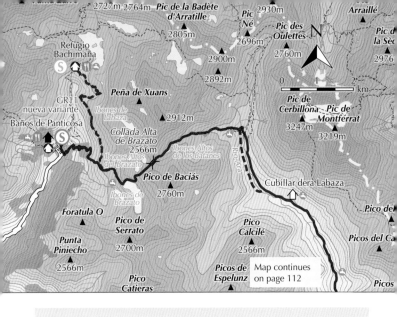

Map continues on page 112

The crossing of the Collada Alta de Brazato, another spectacular alpine pass, would be rather daunting for the inexperienced in bad weather. In good weather this is still a long, high mountain hike.

Head into Baños de Panticosa from the refuge and leave up the steps at the east of the resort. Pass a few ruins and turn left along a track and then, at a switchback, keep straight on along a good path. This well-graded path is in shade if you make an early morning start. Ignore the GR11 nueva variante (see variant route description in Stage 14) coming in from the left, cross a pipeline (2205m, **1hr 55min**) and follow a well-marked trail. The path goes NE up a boulderfield and then veers right (SE) to reach the dam of the **Ibón dero Brazato** (2380m, **40min**). This is your first water on the climb.

Veer left along the northern shore of the reservoir and then follow the path as it switchbacks north to reach the western shoulder of Pico de Baziás (**25min**). The GR11 now contours across a boulderfield to reach **Collada Alta de Brazato** (2566m, **20min**). Follow the small path NE down the valley, passing left of the tiny Ibones Altos de los Batanes on boulderfields. Cross the outlet of the third tarn and continue on easier terrain to a grassy area (**50min**). Good campsites with water at 2150m.

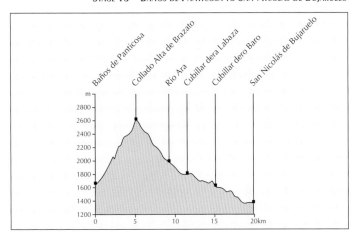

Cross the stream and continue descending the left bank, recrossing lower down to reach the Río Ara (2000m, **30min**). This river could be awkward to cross during snowmelt or after rain. It is safer to cross about 100m further downstream where there is a slight levelling off of the river. Don't be afraid to get your feet wet; it's safer than boulder-hopping. If desperate stay on the western bank to reach a bridge in 1.5km.

The shallow water of Rio Ara at the Puente de Bujaruelo attracts many tourists

Continue down the left-hand side of the river to a small stone hut, **Cubillar dera Labaza** (**35min**), a good emergency shelter. You are now in cow country and good campsites are in short supply. Continue down the left-hand bank to **Cubillar dero Bado** (**1hr**), another basic stone hut (four places), at the end of a track. Follow the track down the left-hand side of the valley, turning sharp left at a junction and pass through a delightful grassy area beside the river. Camping is not allowed. You soon reach the medieval bridge at **San Nicolás de Bujaruelo** (1338m, **1hr**). The Refugio de Bujaruelo with campground and car park is across the bridge.

Refugio de Bujaruelo has full refuge facilities and is open from about 1 March to 2 November. The campground is open from June to September. If you need to get to Torla to resupply, it will probably be relatively easy to catch a ride with one of the people who came up for the day.

FACILITIES ON STAGE 15

Refugio de Bujaruelo: tel 974 486 412 www.refugiodebujaruelo.com

STAGE 16

San Nicolás de Bujaruelo to Refugio de Góriz

Start	San Nicolás de Bujaruelo
Finish	Refugio de Góriz
Time	7hr 55min
Distance	24.3km
Total ascent	1270m
Total descent	450m
Difficulty	In this section you are back onto tracks and good paths. The GR11 is well signed and waymarked.
High point	Refugio de Góriz (2160m)
Note	Camping is not allowed in the Ordesa sector of the Ordesa y Monte Perdido National Park. At Refugio de Góriz, camping is limited and strictly regulated. Hikers are left with two options: making a reservation at Góriz or avoiding having to stay at Góriz by splitting Stage 16 and 17. A suggestion for this last option is made in the route description below.

This walk takes you down the canyon of the Garganta de Bujaruelo and up the world-renowned Ordesa Canyon through some of the most magnificent scenery of the Pyrenees. You are in the Parque Nacional de Ordesa y Monte Perdido and will have to share the canyon with hundreds of tourists. Booking is essential at the Refugio de Góriz, and also if you are camping.

A busy dirt road goes down from the refuge to Puente de los Navarros, but fortunately the GR11 is routed along paths on the opposite side of the river. Go back over the medieval bridge, turn right immediately and follow the path along the left-hand bank of Río Ara. Pass a bridge (**45min**) without crossing it. Just across the bridge is **Camping Valle de Bujaruelo**.

> Camping Valle de Bujaruelo has a bunkhouse, cabins, bar-restaurant and small supermarket in addition to camping. The shop stocks 'original' camping gas.

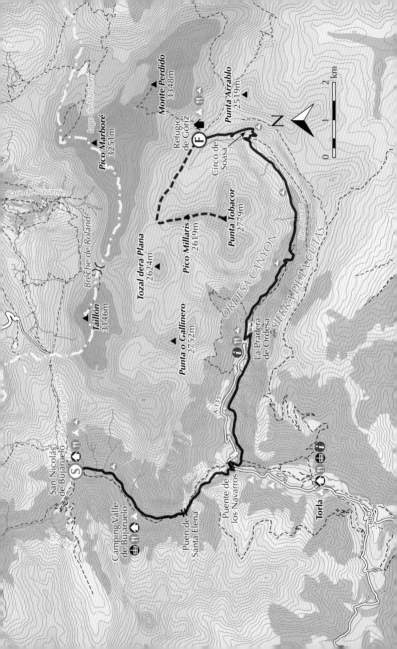

Cave de Gavarnie

Lago de Marboré

Pico Marboré
3251m

Monte Perdido
3348m

Punta Arrablo
2519m

Refugio de Goriz

Circo de Soasa

Brèche de Roland

Taillón
3146m

Tozal dera Plana
2624m

Pico Millaris
2619m

Punta Tobacor
2779m

Punta o Gallinero
2752m

ORDESA CANYON

Río Arazas

SIERRA DE LAS CUTAS

La Pradera
de Ordesa

A-135

RÍO ARA

San Nicolás
de Bujaruelo

Río Ara

Camping Valle
de Bujaruelo

Puen de
Santa Elena

Puente de
los Navarros

Torla

N

0   1   2 km

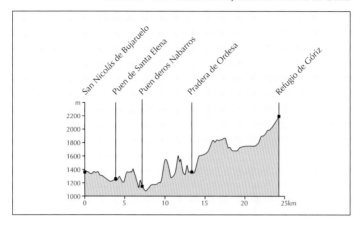

Continue down the left bank of the river to **Puen de Santa Elena (10min)**. Here the dirt road crosses the river, and so do you. Don't be tempted to follow the road as you will miss a spectacular path following ledges along cliff faces high above the river. Turn left after crossing the bridge. At one point a path joins from back right, and further on you fork left (**45min**). Forking right would take you down to San Antón and Torla.

> Torla is a tourist village with supermarkets, bar-restaurants, a large number of hotels, hostals, refugios and casas rurales as well as three campgrounds (listed in the following section). There are buses from Torla into the Ordesa Canyon every 15–30min. There are several good outdoor stores. Intersport stocks all types of camping gas, and 'Coleman-style' gas can be found in most other outdoor shops.

Splitting Stage 16 and 17 in order to avoid staying at Refugio Góriz

The camping restrictions (see information on Góriz at the end of this stage) and the crowded atmosphere at the immensely popular Refugio Góriz might make you want to avoid staying there. You could opt to stay overnight in Torla and take the bus into the Ordesa Canyon the next morning. This would allow you to reach Góriz by noon and push on to Río Bellos where there is a small hut. Camping is possible (and permitted) here too. Higher up along Río Bellos there are also some good places to pitch a tent. Fast hikers could even make it to Refugio de Pineta by the end of the day.

Main route from Puente de los Navarros to Refugio de Góriz

Continue down to the road and turn left. In a few minutes fork left across the old bridge at **Puente de los Navarros** (1060m, **15min**). Turn right under the northern end of the new bridge and descend to cross the Río Arazas on a concrete bridge over some huge but inaccessible swimming holes. Shortly afterwards turn sharp left uphill, then turn left at another junction. Both right turns lead to Torla.

You now climb steadily past an open shelter and fork right past a viewpoint to the Cascade de Tamborrotera; if you visit the viewpoint you can rejoin the GR11 higher up. Continue past a turn to the Cascade de Abetos viewpoint. The next fork left, which you also ignore, is to a bridge with a monument to Lucien Briet.

Frenchman **Lucien Briet** first visited Ordesa in 1891. He was captivated by its outstanding beauty and realised the need to protect the area. He helped promote the cause, which resulted in the creation of the Parque Nacional de Ordesa y Monte Perdido in 1918.

Ignore the next bridge as well, unless you want to visit the bar-restaurant at the roadhead on the opposite side of the river. The GR11 continues on a track along the floor of the valley to reach a path which has been designed for wheelchairs. Turn left along it, crossing a bridge and reaching the National Park Information Office at the **Pradera de Ordesa**, where there is a huge car park (only reachable by bus in summer) (1310m, **1hr 35min**). There are toilets and a water point beside the information centre and a bar-restaurant at the western end of the car park.

Turn right up the track, forking right at a monument, and climb steadily through the woods. Pass a viewpoint for the Cascada de Arripas with a water point (**40min**). If you just continue up the GR11 along the main path, ignoring the viewpoints, you will miss what is probably the most spectacular waterfall in the Pyrenees. Instead follow the sign to Cascada de la Cueva and Cascada del Estrecho. After visiting the Cueva viewpoint continue up the path to a viewpoint at the bottom of Cascada del Estrecho. Then continue up the path to rejoin the GR11. Almost immediately there is an unsigned path forking right to a viewpoint a little below the top of the Cascada del Estrecho. Rejoin the GR11 and soon reach the final two viewpoints for the Cascada del Estrecho.

Continue past another open shelter (**35min**). Eventually the gradient eases at another cascade, Gradas de Soasa (1650m, **30min**), where you pass another water point and the track becomes a tourist path. After a little more climb, you reach the grassy hidden valley of the **Circo de Soasa** (1700m, **30min**). Pass a small hut, intended for emergency use only, and continue to the new bridge at the foot of the Cascada de Caballo ('Horse Tail Falls', 1760m, **25min**). You have now crossed the Greenwich meridian! This is where the tourist path ends, and you are back onto normal mountain paths.

Cross the bridge and take the path signed to Refugio de Góriz, forking left to climb through the first band of crags. Contour left, crossing a small stream (good water, **35min**), before climbing through the second band of crags and continuing easily to **Refugio de Góriz** (2160m, **1hr 10min**).

> The Refugio de Góriz has a full refuge service. It is the only refuge in the immensely popular Ordesa sector of the national park and it is often over-crowded, especially on weekends. The relatively easy climb to Monte Perdido (3355m) is a magnet for many hikers, but the whole Ordesa sector is a popular destination. Camping is strictly regulated here to control the environmental impact; camping in a designated area south-east of the refuge is allowed for a maximum of 50 people, only when the refuge is fully booked, and only with a reservation. Camping costs €15 per person. Elsewhere in the Ordesa sector of the national park, camping (including bivouacking) is prohibited, leaving hikers with no other options but to stay at Góriz or continue on to the Añisclo sector, way past the refuge.

Cascada del Estrecho on the way to Refugio de Góriz (photo: Brian Johnson)

> The refuge offers meals and picnic boxes to campers. If you want to explore the fantastic area around the refuge it is possible to leave your camping equipment in a locker.

> The classic day trip from Refugio de Góriz is the climb of Monte Perdido (3355m), the third highest peak in the Pyrenees. It is spectacular but relatively easy for experienced mountaineers. It is not a route for the casual walker. Equally spectacular, and easier, is the climb to the iconic Brèche de Roland, the col from where you can climb Taillón (3144m). If you want an easier summit, you could climb Punta Tobacor (2779m) via Collado Millaris and Pico Millaris (2619m).

FACILITIES ON STAGE 16

Camping Valle de Bujaruelo: tel 974 486 348

Torla Tourist Office: tel 974 486 378 www.turismo-ordesa.com

Hotel Ballarín and Hostal Alto Aragón: tel 974 486 172
www.hotelballarin.com

Hotel Ordesa: tel 974 486 125 www.hoteles-silken.com

Refugio Lucien Briet: tel 974 486 221 www.refugiolucienbriet.com

Camping Río Ara has a shop and bar-restaurant: tel 974 486 248

Camping San Antón has cabins: tel 974 486 063
www.campingsananton.ordesa.com

Camping Ordesa has cabins, a bar-restaurant and shop: tel 974 117 721
www.campingordesa.es

Refugio de Góriz: tel 974 341 201 www.goriz.es

STAGE 17
Refugio de Góriz to Refugio de Pineta (GR11)

Start	Refugio de Góriz
Finish	Refugio de Pineta
Time	7hr 20min
Distance	12.8km
Total ascent	1135m
Total descent	2055m
Difficulty	The descent from Collado de Arrablo to the Río Bellos is tough and requires great care on the steep descents, especially in rain. Crossing the Barranco Arrablo could be awkward in snowmelt or after heavy rain. The very long (over 1000m) descent from Collado de Añisclo is steep and is both physically and mentally tiring, requiring continuous concentration. Inexperienced hikers and those with knee issues will find that this descent takes considerably longer than suggested below, while experienced hikers with a light backpack may do it faster.
High point	Collado de Añisclo (2453m)

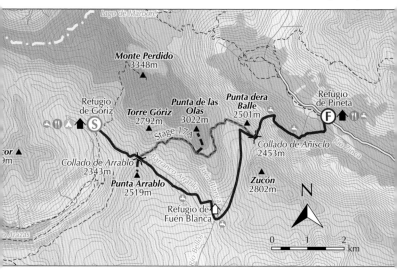

The GR11 used to make its way round the southern side of Punta de las Olas via ledges and gullies, but this route is dangerous in snow and has now been replaced by the described route. If you want to attempt the old route, now named GR11.9, you should check its condition at the Refugio de Góriz – do not attempt it unless you have confirmed that it is free of snow. The lower route followed by the GR11 is still a tough and spectacular route. The routes split 40min after leaving Góriz and meet again at Collado de Añisclo.

The GR11 goes SE from the refuge, passing to the left of the weather station and following a well-marked path to **Collado de Arrablo** (2343m, **40min**). You can climb Punta Arrablo (2519m) from here.

The GR11.9 variant goes off left from here at a signpost. The GR11 follows the path SE, at first down limestone slabs. At 2110m navigate down rocks with the help of a chain. You might spot edelweiss here on the way down. Further on, downclimb several easy rock steps to reach Barranco Arrablo (2329m, **55min**). Cross, possibly getting wet feet, and follow limestone ledges and a path on the other side. Further down, notice **Fuén Blanca**, the waterfall on your left which flows from under the limestone crags of Punta de las Olas. Continue descending

119

Descent route from Collado de Añisclo

past a tiny stone hut (very basic, three places) and down to a narrow bridge over the Río Bellos (1660m, **30min**). Good campsites.

Cross the bridge, turn left and climb steadily with occasional easy rock steps. Occasionally there are good campsites along the river. Fill up your water bottles at about 2200m before leaving the main stream. As you approach the headwall of the canyon, veer right (roughly E). Excellent, dry campsites. Continue to **Collado de Añisclo** (2453m, **2hr 35min**) where the GR11.9 variant rejoins the GR11.

The descent ahead, down a steep rocky slope, looks very intimidating and it would be dangerous to descend without the well-waymarked path. Follow the waymarks carefully! Reach a grassy ridge by a Parque Nacional sign where there is piped water from a small spring (**1hr**). There is space for two small tents here. Shortly afterwards, turn right. The difficulty continues as you descend through the woods with several short but steep rock steps (two with chains) that you need to climb down. Cross several streams (possibly dry) before reaching a junction at the bottom of the descent (**1hr 30min**). Fork right, continue NE and fork left at the next junction. Continue N and cross

120

the flood plain of the Río Zinca, possibly getting wet feet, to reach the **Refugio de Pineta** (1240m, **10min**) which is at a short distance from the A-2611 road.

FACILITIES ON STAGE 17
Refugio de Pineta: tel 974 501 203 www.alberguesyrefugios.com

STAGE 17A
Refugio de Góriz to Refugio de Pineta (GR11.9)

Start	Refugio de Góriz
Finish	Refugio de Pineta
Time	6hr 20min
Distance	11.7km
Total ascent	600m
Total descent	1520m
Difficulty	The GR11.9 variant has some steep exposed parts. The route is just as demanding as the GR11 but the steep parts are more exposed and potentially more dangerous. When back on the GR11, the very long (over 1000m) descent from Collado de Añisclo is steep and both physically and mentally tiring, requiring continuous concentration. You should not attempt this descent if there is snow on the route. Inexperienced hikers and those with knee issues will find that this descent takes considerably longer than suggested below, while experienced hikers with a light backpack may do it faster.
High point	SE ridge of Punta de las Olas (2700m)
Note	For map see Stage 17.

From Collado de Arrablo (**40min**) turn left, climbing roughly NE. Cross a stream (**40min**) and veer right then left to reach about 2600m. The route now veers E, climbing gently to reach 2700m (**50min**) on the south-east ridge of Punta de las Olas before starting to contour easily round the ridge. A cairned route goes off left (**15min**) and gives a reasonably easy climb of Punta de las Olas (3022m, 1hr up, 40min down).

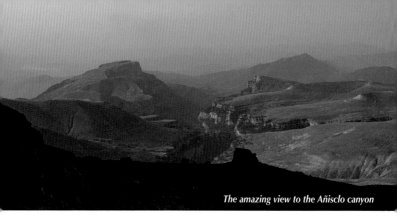
The amazing view to the Añisclo canyon

The route continues to reach the eastern face of the ridge where you pass a small stream flowing out of the rock wall (**15min**). Almost immediately you reach the start of the difficult section. Chains add security as you scramble up a gully and then are essential as you make a strenuous pull up a small rock step. Chains again provide necessary security on an exposed descent of smooth limestone slabs. The going then eases on a gradual descent to the Collata deras Solas (**50min**). Do not descend here. The route climbs slightly, skirting **Punta dera Balle** before descending to **Collado de Añisclo** (**10min**) where you rejoin the GR11.

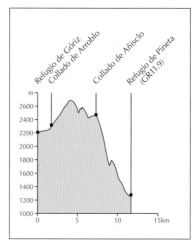

The descent ahead, down a steep rocky slope, looks very intimidating and it would be dangerous to descend without the well-waymarked path. Follow the waymarks carefully! Reach a grassy ridge by a Parque Nacional sign where there is piped water from a small spring (**1hr**). There is space for two small tents here. Shortly afterwards, turn right. The difficulty continues as you descend through the woods with several short but steep rock steps (two with chains) that you need to climb down. Cross several streams (possibly dry) before reaching a junction at the bottom of the descent (**1hr 30min**). Fork right, continue NE and fork left at the next junction. Continue N and cross the flood plain of the Río Zinca, possibly getting wet feet, to reach the **Refugio de Pineta** (1240m, **10min**), which is a short distance from the A-2611 road.

FACILITIES ON STAGE 17A
Refugio de Pineta: tel 974 501 203 www.alberguesyrefugios.com

STAGE 18
Refugio de Pineta to Parzán

Start	Refugio de Pineta
Finish	Parzán
Time	6hr
Distance	19.5km
Total ascent	1370m
Total descent	1480m
Difficulty	This is an easy mountain section.
High point	Collado las Coronetas (2159m)

This stage pales into insignificance compared with the previous few days, but it is still a fine walk with superb views back to the Circo de Pineta and Monte Perdido. The descent down the Río Real valley is on a dirt and asphalt road.

Follow the GR11 NW from Refugio de Pineta on a dirt road along an electricity line. Take the middle path at a complicated junction, reach the A-2166 road and continue NW until you reach Ermita de Nuestra Senora de Pineta (1290m, **25min**), a chapel at the end of the road, immediately before the **Parador de Bielsa Hotel**.

Follow the path to the right of the chapel, signed to Llanos de Larri, and ignore many smaller paths as you climb through the woods to a track. The GR11 shortcuts the switchbacks before following the track again to reach the open pasture of La Larri. Good camping. You soon see a farm building on your right

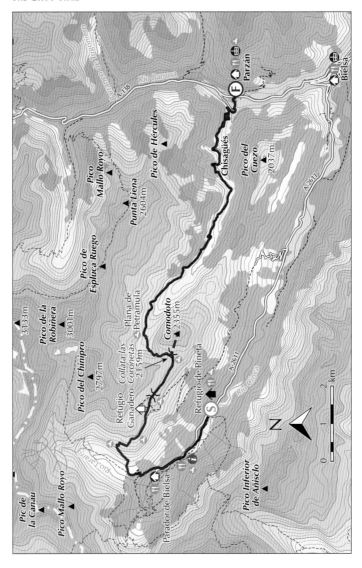

Refugio Ganadero de la Estiva with Monte Perdido,
Cilindro de Marboré and the two Astazou peaks behind

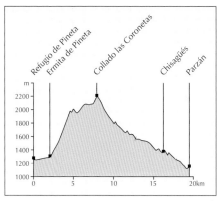

(1560m, **55min**). Continue climbing steeply up and enter a forest. The steepest part is over at 1920m, when the path veers sharply to the right (**55min**). Soon reach the open pasture of the Plana es Corders, where you find, above the path, a cattle trough with spring-fed water running from a tap. From there the path climbs again, crossing three small streams. Cross a track and reach the same track again higher up. If you need a shelter, follow this track to the left for 400m until you reach **Refugio Ganadero de la Estiva** (2100m, at least four places), a comfortable stone hut with spectacular views to Monte Perdido, the Astazous and much more. Otherwise, turn right and follow the track as it crosses a low ridge, Collateta Plana Fonda (**50min**).

Continue into a long grassy bowl, the Plana Fonda, passing another cattle trough with accessible spring water (**10min**). Water and good camping. Shortly afterwards veer left, following waymarks, uphill to the **Collado las Coronetas** (also named Collado de Pietramula, 2159m, **20min**). From here you could make an easy ascent of Comodoto (2355m) to the east of the col by its western ridge (30min up, 20min down).

Descend just left of the dry valley, veering right through large boulders which have fallen from the northern face of Comodoto. Continue down to the bridge over the Barranco Pietramula. Cross the bridge and reach **Plana de Petramula** (1915, **25min**). Pass car parking, reach a dirt road and turn right to go to Parzán, 10km further down. There are frequent water points and camping is possible in several places on the descent. The dirt road becomes a tarmac road shortly before **Chisagüés** (1380m, **1hr 25min**).

> **Chisagüés** was the base for iron and silver mines dating back to the 12th century. Mining reached its peak in the 16th century, when five foundries were working in the valley, and continued until the mid 20th century. Recently new houses have been built here.

Continue down the road. After several switchbacks, the GR11 goes down the road after a last sharp turn left, but you will almost certainly want to visit the facilities at **Parzán**. The shortest way to get there is by turning right onto a path in the sharp turn. A signpost shows the way. Walk down a path, turn right at a farm and walk roughly E through Parzán's narrow streets to go down to the A-138 road (1134m, **35min**).

> **Parzán** is another old mining village with mines dating back to the 11th century. The village was completely destroyed in 1936 during the Spanish Civil War, but has since been rebuilt.

> Hostal-Restaurant La Fuen is situated where you reach the A-138. Across the road is a supermarket and a petrol station where all three types of gas are sold. A larger supermarket is found a little further on the left side of the road. The larger village of Bielsa (restaurants, hotels and shops) is situated 3.5km south of Parzán.

FACILITIES ON STAGE 18

Parador de Bielsa Hotel: tel 974 501 011

Hostal la Fuen: tel 974 501 047 www.lafuenhostal.com

PARZÁN –
LA GUINGUETA D'ÀNEU

Looking down at the Estanys Cap d'Angliós (Stage 22)

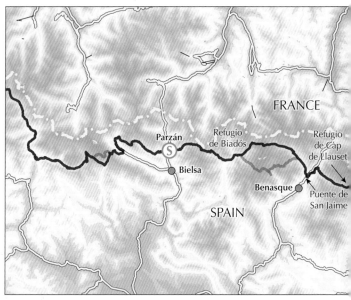

Hikers at Lac deth Cap de Pòrt (Stage 24)

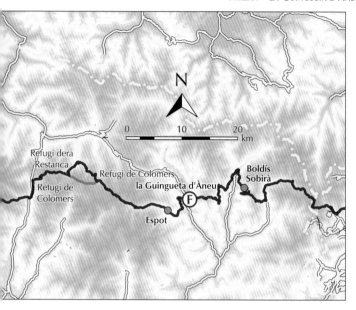

The GR11 now takes you to the very heart of the Pyrenees, passing through the two highest massifs. At first you go to Biadós, where the grey-brown granite Posets (3375m) dominates the landscape. Two beautiful, flower-rich valleys then bring you to the mountain town of Benasque, an ideal place for a break. Benasque is the gateway to the highest part of the Pyrenees: the Maladeta massif with the Aneto, the range's highest mountain, standing at 3404m. The GR11 passes on the south side of the Aneto through the Ballibierna valley with its ancient trees, boulder fields and numerous lakes. Next, follow even more lakes and high mountains in the picturesque Aigüestortes National Park. Section three is a feast for the eyes!

STAGE 19
Parzán to Refugio de Biadós (Viadós)

Start	Parzán
Finish	Refugio de Biadós (Viadós)
Time	7hr
Distance	21.1km
Total ascent	1520m
Total descent	890m
Difficulty	This is an easy day and much of the route is on tracks.
High point	Collado de Urdiceto (2314m)

The climb is rather uninteresting, but the descent is through very scenic terrain.

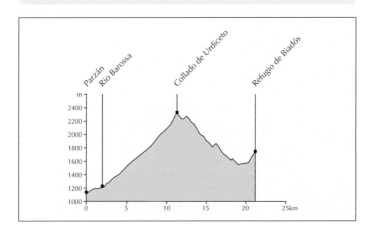

To get back on the GR11 from Parzán, follow the A-138 north, ignore a first road left and turn left at the second road. Walk up this road and turn right onto a track after 200m. Here, you return to the GR11. Soon fork left up a small path, signed to Urdiceto, and climb onto the flat concrete top of a water pipeline. Turn right along it, cross a concrete water channel and veer right then left to continue on

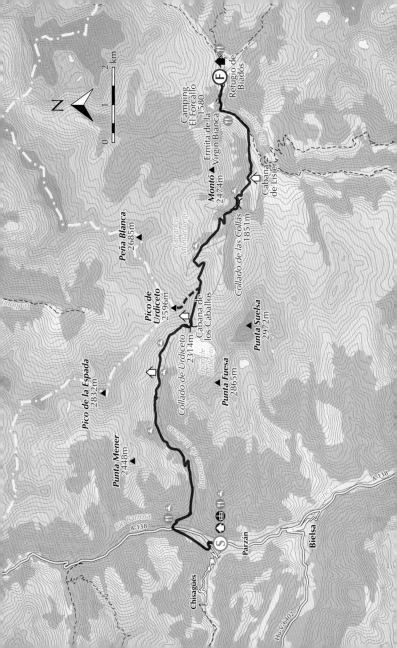

The barns at Biadós with Pico Posets (3375m) behind

top of, or alongside, the buried pipeline. Fork right to go down to the A-138 road (**30min**). Take care not to miss this junction! Cross the A-138 and follow a dirt road on the other side, which soon crosses the Río Barossa. Bar-restaurant La Pleta is on your left. There is a space here where you are allowed to pitch tents. Pass car parking and continue going up the dirt road, with Barranco de Urdiceto well below on your right. After 1.5km up this road there is a good campsite with water in a field on your right. A short side-road gets you to the field. Pass a spring-fed water point (**1hr 30min**), which may be the first water on the climb.

On reaching a sign for 'hydro-electric powerstation', take a shortcut up a concrete track and then turn left up a path at a 'no entry' sign to regain the track beside a small reservoir. Continue up the track, passing a small basic hut (1980m, **50min**), a good emergency shelter. If you intend to camp before the col you should do so somewhere near here. Continue up the track until it starts a large switchback. The GR11 goes straight on along a path where you find your last water until well down the other side of the col. The path rejoins the track just before the **Collado de Urdiceto** (2314m, **55min**).

The track continues up to the Ibón de Urdiceto, but the GR11 veers left to a small stone hut, Cabana de los Caballos (four places) and follows a clear, well-waymarked path, roughly E. The path gains the south-east ridge of Pico de Urdiceto (**20min**); Pico de Urdiceto (2597m) is an easy climb from here (45min up, 25min down).

Descend the grassy ridge until the path veers left (N) at a level spot and descends to the **Barranco Montarruego**. Water and good campsites. The path veers back E and crosses the stream on a bridge (**45min**). Continue E or SE through woods to a meadow with a ruined hut, where a track starts. Follow the track, turning left down a rough path immediately after the first switchback, rejoining the track at a stream. Take another shortcut on the left and then follow the track up to the **Collado de las Collás** (1851m, **45min**).

Follow the track down, shortcutting a series of switchbacks (water point on first switchback) on paths and pass the tiny **Cabana de Lisiert** (good emergency shelter, 1720m, **10min**). Pass left of farm buildings and down to a junction with a dirt road (1540m, **30min**). No camping allowed along this road. Turn left up the road, pass a youth camp and the Ermita de la Virgin Bianca and continue to a bar-restaurant (order meals in advance) and campground at Es Plans.

Camping El Forcallo at Es Plans is only open in July and August.

From here, head left up a well-waymarked path, which shortcuts the switchbacks in the track, to the **Refugio de Biadós** (1760m, **45min**).

Refugio de Biadós is open weekends from April to June, and is open every day from mid June to mid October.

FACILITIES ON STAGE 19
Bar-restaurant La Pleta: tel 656 946 565
Camping El Forcallo: tel 974 341 613
Refugio de Biadós: tel 974 341 613 www.viados.es, www.alberguesyrefugios.com

STAGE 20

Refugio de Biadós to Puente de San Jaime (GR11)

Start	Refugio de Biadós
Finish	Puente de San Jaime
Time	6hr 45min
Distance	20.1km
Total ascent	940m
Total descent	1450m
Difficulty	A long but easy route over well-defined paths.
High point	Puerto de Chistau (2572m)

The GR11 follows a relatively easy route along paths to the Refugio d'Estós over the Puerto de Chistau, joining the sunny, flower-rich valleys of Añes Cruces and Estós, and then heading down tracks to Puente de San Jaime. In good weather, it is worth considering taking the longer and tougher two-day variant GR11.2, which follows the southern section of the Circuito de los Tres Refugios, and which promises much more spectacular landscape. It circumnavigates the Posets massif and rejoins the GR11 above Puente de San Jaime.

The GR11 and GR11.2 are used for the **Gran Trail Aneto-Posets**, which circumnavigates the two highest peaks in the Pyrenees: Aneto (3404m) and the Posets (3375m). This 114km trail, with 6650m of climb, is the route of an annual race held in late July. You probably want to avoid being in the area around this time! www.trail-aneto.com

Go down a few metres in front of the refugio, cross a stream and climb gently E along the Bordas de Viados (meadows with barns). Ignore the path to Collado de Eriste at a junction (this path is the variant GR11.2), turn left and follow the path that turns into the valley of the Barranco de Añescruzes. Follow the path NE, notice a cabin on your left above, and further notice the **Cabana de Añescruzes** (four places) on a bluff ahead of you. Go around this bluff on the right to Pleta d'Añes Cruces, the junction of three streams (2080m, **1hr 40min**). Water and camping. Cross all three streams and follow the path which climbs steeply up

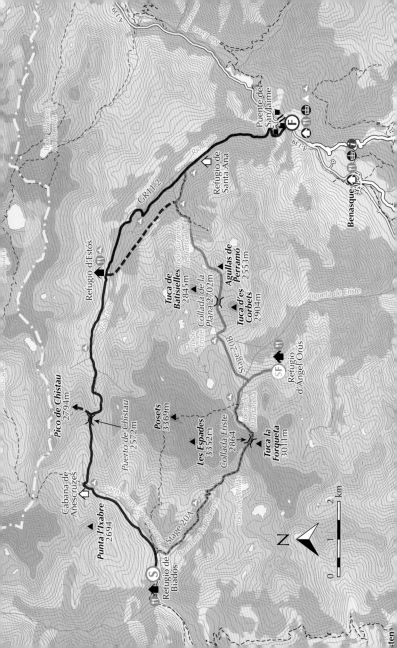

Refugio Estós

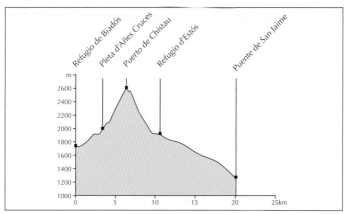

the valley to the E. Continue to reach the **Puerto de Chistau** (2572m, **1hr 35min**), which gives access to the Valle de Estós. You could climb Pico de Chistau (2794m) by its south-west ridge from here (25min up, 15min down).

Veer right and descend easily on a path down scree on the right of the valley to cross a stream. If you plan to camp here, do so well above the **Refugio d'Estós**, as camping below the refuge is prohibited. You then cross the Río Estós before descending the left-hand side. The path is well above the stream by the time you reach the Refugio d'Estós (1890m, **1hr 30min**). The refuge is not visible from above and only comes into view when you are very near.

Refugio d'Estós, a popular manned refuge with full facilities, is open all year.

Continue down the left-hand side of the valley, soon forking left at a junction with the GR11.2, crossing to the right-hand side at a bridge and past a herder's hut, Cabana del Turmo. Follow the dirt road which starts from this hut. After a few minutes the GR11 forks (**1hr 10min**) left down a path. This short deviation from the dirt road allows you to view the cascades in Las Gorgas Galantes. Turn left on rejoining the dirt road. Pass a junction and soon pass a spring with piped water. Continue past the **Refugio de Santa Ana (15min)**.

As you approach the bottom of the descent turn sharp right, pass two car parks, then turn right, signed to Hostal Parque Natural, before forking right down a path. Cross the old bridge over the Río Esera to arrive at Camping Aneto in **Puente de San Jaime (35min**, 1250m). Camping Ixeia is 10min along the Stage 21 route.

Puente de San Jaime has a hostal and two campgrounds: Camping Aneto has a bar-restaurant, supermarket, cabins and bunkhouse accommodation, and the shop stocks 'original' and 'easy-clic' camping gas; Camping Ixeia has a bar-restaurant, cabins and a bunkhouse.

The tourist resort of Benasque is 3km to the south-west and has all services, including a mountain equipment shop which stocks all types of camping gas. There are buses in summer from Benasque to Puente de San Jaime continuing up the dirt road all the way to the Refugio de Coronas.

FACILITIES ON STAGE 20

Refugio d'Estós: tel 974 344 515 www.alberguesyrefugios.com/

Hostal Parque Natural and bar-restaurant: tel 974 344 584 www.hostalparquenatural.com

Camping Aneto: tel 974 551 141 www.campinganeto.com

Camping Ixeia: tel 974 552 129 www.campingixeia.es

Benasque Oficina de Turismo: tel 974 551 289 www.turismobenasque.com

Refugio d'Ángel Orús: tel 974 344 044 www.alberguesyrefugios.com

STAGE 20A
Day 1: Refugio de Biadós to Refugio d'Ángel Orús (GR11.2)

Start	Refugio de Biadós
Finish	Refugio d'Ángel Orús
Time	5hr 35min
Distance	10.2km
Total ascent	1195m
Total descent	840m
Difficulty	The path traverses steep slopes and care will be needed in places. In a high-snow year, snow can linger well into summer on the descent. Day 1 of the variation GR11.2 takes you over the 2864m Collada Eriste, but the ascent is as easy as you are likely to find on such a high pass. The route is easy to follow in good weather but not recommended for bad weather.
High point	Collada Eriste (2864m)
Note	For map see Stage 20.

Follow the GR11 for **10min** then fork right (signed) and cross the Río Zinqueta and follow the path through a delightful wood and meadow high above the left bank of the Barranco la Ribereta. After crossing the Barranco las Tuertas (**1hr 25min**) the gradient steepens. The last camping before the col is as you reach the treeline. Eventually reach a signpost (**35min**) where the tourist path veers right to Ibón de Millás. The GR11.2 heads steeply uphill on a faint path. The gradient eases (**50min**) and climbs ESE up the long valley to the obvious col, **Collada Eriste** (2864m,

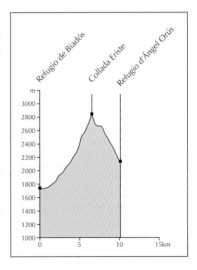

Bivouac at Ibón Llardaneta

1hr). Tuca La Forqueta (3011m), north of the col, is a relatively easy climb from here (30min up, 20min down).

Head down E, veering NE, to go left of Ibón Llardaneta and continue down the well-marked path. The first good camping on the descent is on the left at about 2460m. You soon cross a bridge over the Barranco Llardaneta and descend to a junction with a signpost (2370m, **1hr 15min**). If you don't need the refuge you can turn left here and start Stage 20b. Otherwise veer right and descend to **Refugio d'Ángel Orús** (2112m, **30min**), situated at the foot of the east ridge of Forcau Alto (2865m).

You could climb Posets (3375m), one of the easier 3000m peaks, from the refuge. The path goes off left as you descend from Ibón Llardaneta.

Refugio d'Ángel Orús is a manned refuge with full refuge facilities.

STAGE 20B

Day 2: Refugio d'Ángel Orús to Puente de San Jaime (GR11.2)

Start	Refugio d'Ángel Orús
Finish	Puente de San Jaime
Time	6hr 10min
Distance	13.9km
Total ascent	720m
Total descent	1585m
Difficulty	Paths are easy to follow but this hike involves a good deal of rough terrain.
High point	Collada de la Plana (2702m)
Note	For map, see Stage 20.

Return to the signed junction at 2370m where you turned right to go to Refugio d'Ángel Orús on the Day 1 walk (detailed in Stage 20A) (**45min**). Fork right and cross the Barranco Llardaneta and traverse to the dilapidated Cabana de Llardana. The path gradually climbs and veers left to reach the outlet stream from Ibón Eriste (2394m, **1hr**) where you will find the last camping before the col. Cross and veer right before climbing easily ENE to arrive at the Ibón de la Plana. The path goes above

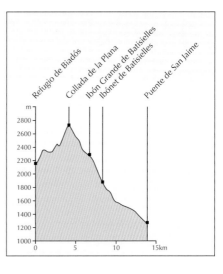

the left bank and up to the obvious **Collada de la Plana** (2702m, **1hr 10min**). Good legal campsites are in short supply on the descent.

Follow the path, easily aiming to the left of the **Agullas de Perramó** (2553m), the peak to the east which splits the valley in descent. At the foot of this peak the route

Río Estós (photo: Brian Johnson)

heads steeply down (N) and care is needed to follow the cairns and waymarks. The gradient eases, but the terrain remains rough as you pass to the right of three small lakes and descend to the **Ibón Grande de Batisielles** (2209m, **1hr 20min**). The path now improves as it descends to the tiny Ibónet de Batisielles (1861m, **30min**) where there is a small woodshed that may serve as an emergency shelter.

There is now a choice of routes to rejoin the GR11. You could continue along the GR11.2, forking left, to reach the Refugio d'Estós in about 90min. But the more logical choice is the more direct route, which forks right and follows the tourist path signed to Cabana de Santa Ana. Reach the track (1552m, **35min**) descending from the Refugio d'Estós and turn right along the GR11. Continue past the **Refugio de Santa Ana**.

FACILITIES ON STAGE 20B

Hostal Parque Natural and bar-restaurant: tel 974 344 584 www.hostalparquenatural.com

Camping Aneto: tel 974 551 141 www.campinganeto.com

Camping Ixeia: tel 974 552 129 www.campingixeia.es

Benasque Oficina de Turismo: tel 974 551 289 www.turismobenasque.com

Refugio d'Ángel Orús: tel 974 344 044 www.alberguesyrefugios.com

As you approach the bottom of the descent turn sharp right, pass two car parks, then turn right, signed to Hostal Parque Natural, before forking right down a path where you arrive at **Puente de San Jaime** (1250m, **45min**). Camping Aneto is right by the bridge and Camping Ixeia is 10min along the route for Stage 21.

STAGE 21

Puente de San Jaime to Refugio de Cap de Llauset

Start	Puente de San Jaime
Finish	Refugio de Cap de Llauset
Time	7hr 10min
Distance	16.9km
Total ascent	1570m
Total descent	395m
Difficulty	This is a rough, tough stage with a lot of boulderfield, but fortunately the waymarking is excellent. Snow can linger over the pass well into summer.
High point	Collado de Ballibierna (2732m)
Note	There is a regular bus service from Benasque, via Puente de San Jaime, to Puente de Coronas from July to early September.

This stage starts with a long walk up a dirt road. Fortunately, the only traffic on the road is the bus which operates from Benasque to Puente de Coronas. Camping is very limited before Puente de Coronas. After this you cross one of the toughest passes on the GR11.

Go over the old bridge and turn left up the riverbank. Go under the road bridge and turn left along a dirt road, passing a track to Camping Ixeia. Take a short-cut left just after the first switchback then turn left along the eastern shore of the **Embalse de Paso Nuevo** to reach a major junction (**50min**). Turn right up the concrete road. There is frequent water on the climb ahead. Some 15min later the GR11 takes a steep shortcut to the right, but you might prefer to stay on the dirt road for a steady climb. Turn right after returning to the road as it climbs steadily up a gorge lined with granite cliffs. Pass the **Refugio d'el Quillón** (six places),

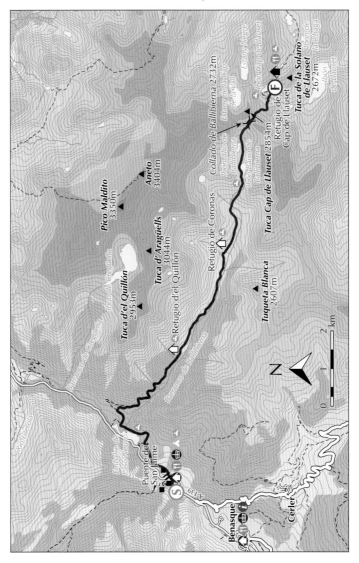

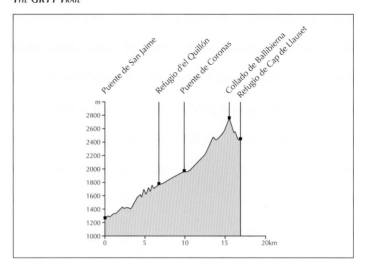

just above you on the left (**1hr 30min**). Continue to the roadhead at the Puente de Coronas (**20min**) with the large **Refugio de Coronas** (10 places, emergency phone) close by. Water. Camping is not allowed in the vicinity of the bothy, but there are plenty of good campsites further up the valley.

Follow the well-waymarked track roughly E from the refuge and fork right a little further on, signed Ibones de Ballibierna. The track becomes a path before you reach a flat area, Pleta de Llosas (**1hr 20min**). Fork right, still following the signs to Ibones de Ballibierna, cross a bridge and climb a sparsely wooded ridge to cross the outlet of the **Ibón Baixo de Ballibierna**, which is followed to the lake (2440m, **45min**). The route from here is complex, rough and tough with boulderfields and crags. Continue along the northern shore of the lower lake and up the ridge to the east to reach the **Ibón Alto de Ballibierna** (**50min**). Camping is possible at this corrie lake. Continue up a combination of path, boulderfield and possibly snowfield to reach the **Collado de Ballibierna** (2732m, **50min**).

The descent starts down the centre of the valley, down a boulderfield or snowfield, before veering right and following a well-waymarked, complex route down to a signpost by the main stream (2410m). At 2520m a small path goes right to Tuca de Vallibierna (3067m, 2hr up, 1hr 30min down) over a route which involves a relatively easy but spectacular ridge walk. This is not a route for hikers with vertigo! Cross the stream and climb to the **Refugio de Cap de Llauset** (2425m, **45min**), a modern refuge with full refuge facilities.

Looking back at Ibóns de Ballibierna from Collado de Ballibierna

FACILITIES ON STAGE 21

Refugio de Cap de Llauset: tel 974 120 400
www.refugiocapdellauset.es, www.alberguesyrefugios.com

STAGE 22

Refugio de Cap de Llauset to Refugi de Conangles

Start	Refugio de Cap de Llauset
Finish	Refugi de Conangles
Time	3hr 45min
Distance	10km
Total ascent	240m
Total descent	1110m
Difficulty	Although mainly downhill, this is a tough section with boulderfields to cross and a steep descent.
High point	Collet dels Estanyets (2524m)

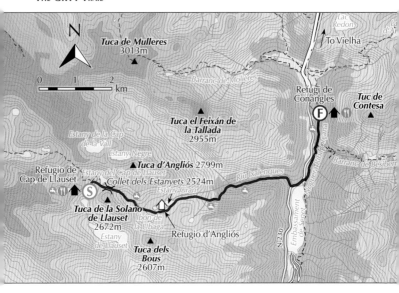

> The magnificent scenery continues on the long, tough descent to the Refugi de Conangles.

At the east side of the refuge, follow the waymarks NE to the south shore of Ibón Cap de Llauset (**10min**). Excellent campsites on the north-western shore. Follow the path round the southern shore and head SE to the **Collet dels Estanyets** (2524m, **25min**). Descend down a boulderfield to the three Estanys Cap d'Angliós and along the southern shore, mainly on boulderfield. Continue down grassy slopes to a sign just before the **Refugio d'Angliós** (eight places, 2220m, **50min**). This wooden hut is located a little left of the waymarked path. Water.

The path continues down to and along the southern shore of the **Estany Gran**, before descending a well-waymarked rough path high above the right-hand bank of the Barranco d'Angliós. A steep descent leads to a path junction, with signpost and picnic table, beside the Ríu Ixalenques (**1hr 15min**). Turn right along an easier path for a pleasant descent of the right-hand side of the river. At the bottom, steps lead right to the main road (N-230) (1460m, **30min**) at the northern end of the Embassament de Senet.

A Spanish youth group at Refugio d'Angliós

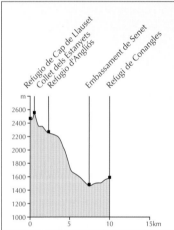

Turn left across the road bridge and follow the road until there is a track on the right. A signpost shows the way. Take the track, immediately crossing a bridge and turning left. A waymarked combination of track, path and river bed leads through wood and meadow along the Noguera Ribagorçana. At the Barranc de Besiberri you need to head a little upstream to cross the bridge before descending again to the river. Continue until you pass a picnic area with large car park on your left. Keep going up a tarmac track and soon reach the **Refugi de Conangles** on your left (1555m, **35min**).

Refugi de Conangles, with full refuge facilities, is open all year. In recent years, the refugio has regularly been fully booked by youth groups. If this is the case, there is no accommodation or food available. Booking well in advance is recommended.

Alternative accommodation can be found in Vielha. The only quick option to get there is by catching a ride to get through the road tunnel.

FACILITIES ON STAGE 22

Refugi de Conangles: tel 696 649 871 www.lacentralderefugis.com, www.refusonline.com

---

STAGE 23

Refugi de Conangles to Refugi dera Restanca

Start	Refugi de Conangles
Finish	Refugi dera Restanca
Time	5hr 20min
Distance	12km
Total ascent	970m
Total descent	515m
Difficulty	Most of this section is on good well-waymarked mountain paths, with only a little difficult terrain.
High point	Pòrt de Rius (2355m)

The route passes through magnificent granite scenery. If the weather is good and you have time to spare, it is worth following the alternative route via Lac de Mar.

Return to the track and continue until you cross the Barranc de Lac Redon, with signpost. Turn right up the left-hand side of the stream to another signpost at a path junction (**25min**). The path left takes you to the Hospital de Vielha, which is no longer a refuge. The GR11 turns right and follows a well-waymarked route to cross the Barranc de Lac Redon. There are camping opportunities and water early on this ascent. As you climb the path veers left (N then W) before reaching a path junction (**1hr 30min**). The left path goes to Lac Redon but the GR11 switchbacks sharp right (NE) and climbs easily up to the **Pòrt de Rius** (2355m, **50min**). The path now stays fairly level as it traverses above a pond and then along the northern shore of **Lac de Rius**. Camping possible, but better sites just ahead. Cross the often dry outlet stream at the eastern end of the lake (**35min**).

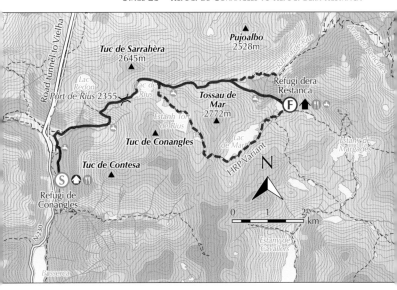

Early morning at Lac de Rius

The **Haute Randonnée Pyrénéenne** (HRP) goes off right here to the Estanh Tòrt de Rius and the Lac de Mar to rejoin the GR11 at the Refugi dera Restanca. It takes about 4hr to reach the Refugi dera Restanca from the Lac de Rius by this magnificent variant to the GR11.

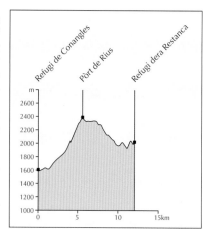

Follow the path down the right bank of the often dry Ribèra de Rius. A little further on you pass a crag on your right, out of which a little spring flows from a small pipe. Just below the spring is a flat area with excellent campsites (**10min**). Continue easily down the right-hand side of the valley until the path forks at a signed junction (1943m, **45min**).

If you don't intend to visit the Refugi dera Restanca but are intending to take the official (northern) route of the GR11 on Stage 24, you could **shortcut** by forking left from here to rejoin the GR11 at the Cabana de Rius.

If you require the Refugi dera Restanca, or if you are taking the highly rec- ommended GR11.18 variation on Stage 24, you should fork right here. The path now becomes rougher as it climbs over a ridge and descends to a stream (**30min**). It then climbs a second ridge, under a power line. From the ridge it is just a few minutes' descent to the **Refugi dera Restanca** (2010m, **35min**) at the eastern end of the dam. Camping is not allowed in the vicinity of the refuge.

Refugi dera Restanca, a manned refuge with full refuge facilities, is open roughly from June to late September. A central booking system operates for this and other refuges in the area.

The Refugi dera Restanca is one of the refuges on the popular Carros de Foc ('Chariots of Fire') tour in the Parc Nacional de Aigüestortes i Estany de Sant Maurici, which is a tour of nine manned refuges in the Park: Amitges, Saboredo, Colomèrs, Restanca, Ventosa i Calvell, Estany Llong, Colomina, Josep Maria Blanc and Ernest Mallafré. For those with a competitive urge, the

Carros de Foc Sky Runner takes place at the beginning of September, when the challenge is to complete the route in 24hr. www.carrosdefoc.com

FACILITIES ON STAGE 23
Refugi dera Restanca: tel 608 036 559 www.lacentralderefugis.com/refugios/restanca Central reservations: tel 973 641 681 www.refusonline.com

STAGE 24
Refugi dera Restanca to Refugi de Colomèrs (GR11)

Start	Refugi dera Restanca
Finish	Refugi de Colomèrs
Time	5hr 5min
Distance	13.9km
Total ascent	985m
Total descent	860m
Difficulty	Easy. Much of the route is along tracks.
High point	Coret d'Oelhacrestada (2475m)

The official GR11 follows mainly roads and is longer and less scenic than the GR11.18 variation (see Stage 24A). It is highly recommended to follow the GR11.18.

Return across the dam and turn right down a good path to reach a track at **Cabana de Rius** (4 places, basic, **40min**). Turn right and continue descending, passing a track on the left to a picnic site beside the river. Shortly afterwards reach another junction (1420m, **25min**) and turn right, signed to Montcasau (no GR waymarks). Follow a good track which switchbacks up the hillside, eventually reaching a junction (**1hr 10min**). Turn sharp right, signed to Montcasau, and when this track ends (**20min**) head up a steep path to the left of the outlet stream from the **Estany de Montcasau**. Probably your last water until just before the end of the section.

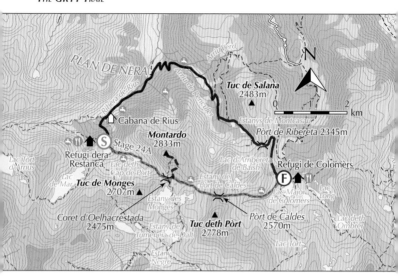

Reach the dam (**30min**) and follow a good path above the left-hand side of the two lakes. This path switchbacks easily up the steep slopes to the **Pòrt de Ribereta** (2345m, **1hr**).

The descent starts to the left before switchbacking down the steep slope and turning right (S) on a rising traverse to an unnamed col above Lac Major de Colomèrs (2207m, **50min**). Descend to a junction with

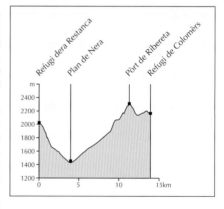

the GR11.18 and turn left, then right, to the **Refugi de Colomèrs** (2135m, **10min**).

Refugi de Colomèrs, a manned refuge with full refuge facilities, is open from early June to mid September. See website for opening times outside this period. Central booking operates for this refuge.

Estany de Mangades and Estany del Port de Caldes with Tuc de Molière behind

FACILITIES ON STAGE 24

Refugi de Colomèrs: tel 973 253 008 www.refugicolomers.com

Reservation centre: tel 973 641 681 www.refusonline.com

STAGE 24A

Refugi dera Restanca to Refugi de Colomèrs (by Port de Caldes, GR11.18)

Start	Refugi dera Restanca
Finish	Refugi de Colomèrs
Time	3hr 50min
Distance	7.1km
Total ascent	695m
Total descent	565m
Difficulty	There are long boulderfields to cross and care will be needed when navigating in bad weather.
High points	Coret d'Oelhacrestada (2475m), Port de Caldes (2570m)
Note	From Coret d'Oelhacrestada to Port de Caldes the route is marked by yellow posts, otherwise it's GR waymarks backed up by cairns. The route enters a national park where camping is strictly prohibited. For map see Stage 24.

Dam at Refugi dera Restanca (photo: Brian Johnson)

This variant route is shorter and offers better landscapes than the official GR11 route.

Leave the hut at its south-eastern side and hike up the left path (the path along the shoreline is the route taken by the HRP, descending from the Lac de Mar). Soon climb up steeply along a stream to **Lac deth Cap de Pòrt** (2230m, **40min**). Cross a dam and head along the northern shore of this beautiful lake, hiking up a well-waymarked boulderfield to the **Col de Crestada** (also named Coret de Oelhacrestada, 2475m, **1hr 5min**), where you enter the Aigüestortes i Estany de Sant Maurici National Park. Camping is strictly prohibited here. Follow yellow poles roughly E, which climb to an unnamed col to the ESE (2520m, **15min**).

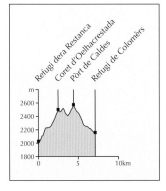

Shortly below Col de Crestada a signpost shows you the way up a cairned path towards the south-east ridge of **Montardo**. Upon reaching the ridge follow a path left to the summit of Montardo (45min up, 30min down).

From the unnamed col, follow well-defined paths ESE towards the obvious col ahead, Port de Caldes. On the way you descend to the southern end of the Estany del Port de Caldes (**15min**) before climbing easily to the **Port de Caldes** (2570m, **35min**). From here there are again GR11 waymarks. The path now descends roughly E to reach a stream. Descend the left-hand side of this stream until just above Lac Major de Colomèrs. Turn right, at a sign, to the large modern **Refugi de Colomèrs** (2135m, **1hr**) on the western shore of the reservoir. The old refuge on the western end of the dam is now closed and locked.

The area north of Lac Major de Colomèrs, in between the hut and the Cirque de Colomèrs, probably has the highest density of lakes and ponds in the Pyrenees. It is worth exploring this area for the exceptional views, and also for the butterflies, damselflies and dragonflies. There is a shorter circular circuit (yellow marks, 2hr) and also a long circuit (red marks, 4hr) starting from Refugi de Colomèrs.

Refugi de Colomèrs, a manned refuge with full refuge facilities, is open from early June to mid September. See website for opening times outside this period. Central booking operates for this refuge.

FACILITIES ON STAGE 24

Refugi de Colomèrs: tel 973 253 008 www.refugicolomers.com

Reservation centre: tel 973 641 681 www.refusonline.com

STAGE 25

Refugi de Colomèrs to Espot

Start	Refugi de Colomèrs
Finish	Espot
Time	6hr
Distance	19km
Total ascent	525m
Total descent	1330m
Difficulty	A relatively easy section, but navigation could be tricky in bad weather.
High point	Pòrt de Ratèra (2590m)

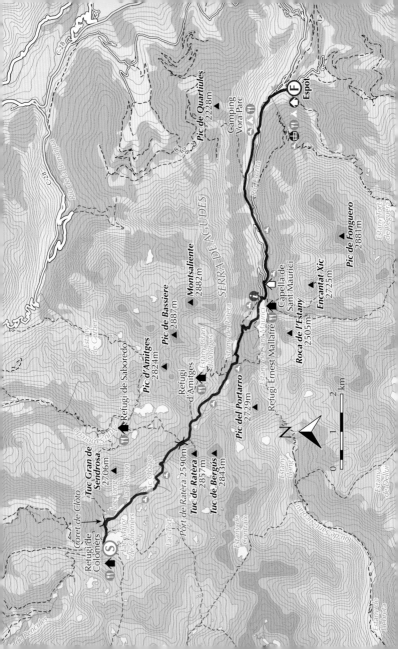

This is a magnificent walk through the Parc Nacional d'Aigüestortes i Estany de Sant Maurici. The area around the Estany de Sant Maurici – with its high, jagged peaks and lower mountain tops dressed with pines and large waterfalls – is understandably popular with hikers.

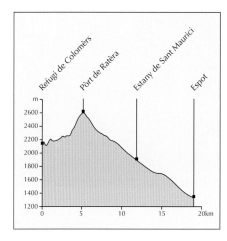

From the new refuge, take the path to the old refuge at the western end of the dam and cross the dam. Descend a little at the end of the dam then veer right (E) and climb to a pass, **Coret de Clòto** (**30min**). There are plenty of good campsites and water all the way up to the Pòrt de Ratèra. The Pòrt de Ratèra is the obvious col to the SE. From here, you head slightly right – contouring roughly SE and ignoring side turns – to reach **Lac Long**.

Follow the path along the south-western shore of Lac Long and Lac Redon to reach **Lac Obago** (**35min**). Cabana d'Estanh Obago, on your left just before reaching the lake, is a ruin. Turn left 100m past the south-western end of Lac Obago, ignoring old waymarks which fork right away from the lake, and follow the path round the lake until you are close to the south-eastern end of it. There the clear path heads SE up to the **Pòrt de Ratèra**. This broad, grassy pass has a false col, then a slight drop with a path (GR211-4) going off left to the Refugi de Saboredo (30min) before the high point (2590m, **1hr 25min**). Tuc de Ratèra to the right of the col is an easy climb. Follow the cairned path which climbs the eastern face of Tuc de Ratèra, and when the path reaches the rocky summit ridge turn left to the summit (40min up, 25min down).

The descent is marked by wooden posts with GR markings. Follow the path, initially contouring E, ignoring any side turns, including a left fork to the Refugi d'Amitges.

Refugi d'Amitges is a popular manned refuge with full refuge facilities.

Els Encantats, the iconic twin peaks of the national park

Continue to descend, mainly SE, to the upper waters of the Ríu de Ratèra and follow the stream down, crossing it several times over wooden bridges before reaching a signed junction (**55min**). Fork right and pass left of the Estany de les Obagues de Ratera before crossing the stream again and reaching a dirt road (**20min**). Turn left, ignore a sharp left turn to the Refugi d'Amitges and pass along the southern shore of the Estany de Ratèra. Cross a bridge across the Ríu de Ratèra.

After 50m a path goes down on your right while the GR11 continues on the dirt road. It is highly recommended that you follow the path to the right, which goes down to a large waterfall (the 'Salt de Ratèra') and further on offers splendid views over **Estany de Sant Maurici**, with the twin peaks Els Encantats behind. The path rejoins the GR11 1.5km after leaving the dirt road at the east end of the lake. Both options are about the same length.

A short distance from where the two paths meet is the National Park Information Office in a small wooden building (1920m, **40min**). The dirt road heading E from here goes to Espot, but the GR11 continues roughly S past the lake, passing public toilets on the way. Follow a dirt road, soon veering E. After a few minutes a track goes off right to Refugi Ernest Mallafré.

Refugi Ernest Mallafré is a manned refuge with full refuge facilities.

The GR11 continues roughly E. Pass the **Capella de Sant Maurici** (**10min**), which has a water point, a shady seating area and a small hut. Soon after the chapel, fork right down a path. Keep straight on across a tarmac road as you continue down the left-hand side of the Ríu Escrita. Fork left (**30min**) along a grassy track. After a right fork you leave the Aigüestortes i Estany de Sant Maurici National Park and the track becomes a path which you follow until it eventually crosses the Ríu Escrita on a bridge (**35min**). Turn left down the road, passing a dirt road to Camping Vora Parc. A little further on you find Camping Riu Gelat on your right. As you enter **Espot**, stay immediately right of the river. Camping Solau is across the river. Continue down to reach the centre of Espot (1330m, **20min**).

Espot is a tourist village with a good selection of hotels, casas rurales, campgrounds, shops, bars and restaurants (some listed below). The small outdoor store stocks all types of camping gas. Land Rover taxis take tourists from Espot to Estany de Sant Maurici and Estany d'Amitges. www.taxisespot.com

FACILITIES ON STAGE 25

Refugi d'Amitges: tel 973 250 109 www.amitges.com

Refugi Ernest Mallafré: tel 973 250 118

Central reservations: tel 973 641 681 www.refusonline.com

Hotel Roca Blanca: tel 973 624 156 www.hotelrocablanca.com

Els Encantats Hotel: tel 680 276 907 www.hotelencantats.com

Hotel Roya: tel 973 624 040 www.hotelroya.net

Hotel Saurat: tel 973 624 162 www.hotelsaurat.com

Camping Vora Parc has a bar-restaurant, mini-market and luxury tents: tel 973 624 108 www.voraparc.com

Camping Riu Gelat: tel 696 585 365 www.campingriugelat.com

Camping Solau: tel 666 138 871 www.campingsolau.com

Camping La Torre: tel 973 624 160 www.campinglatorre.com

STAGE 26
Espot to La Guingueta d'Àneu

Start	Espot
Finish	La Guingueta d'Àneu
Time	2hr 30min
Distance	9.7km
Total ascent	250m
Total descent	600m
Difficulty	Easy
High point	Estaís (1400m)

This is not much more than a 'rest day'. The next few days are in the foothills of the Pyrenees and there is a break from alpine terrain until the crossing into Andorra. Water is scarce in these dry hills.

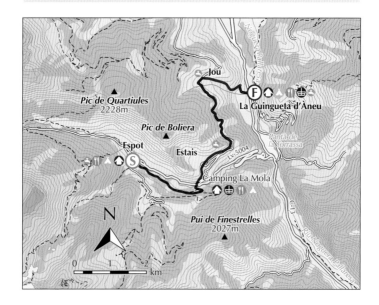

The river Noguera Pallaresa near La Guingueta d'Àneu

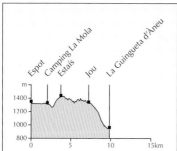

Leave Espot down the street immediately right of the river. Cross a bridge and turn left immediately. Follow a track along Riu Escrita. After 15min pass a covered seating area and shortly afterwards fork left down a path then turn sharp left down a rough track. Cross Riu Escrita by a bridge and climb to the main road (1250m, **35min**). **Camping La Mola** is on your left.

Camping La Mola also has a bar-restaurant, supermarket and cabins.

Cross the road and follow the path opposite. This path shortcuts the switchbacks on the road to Jou. As you cross a ridge turn left up a track which leads to **Estaís** (1400m, **40min**). The waymarks going left from the church square take you on a tour of the hamlet before exiting E from the northern corner along a tarmac road. You soon fork left along an old path which contours, rounding the ridge, and then gradually descends to meet the road to Jou (**15min**).

161

Turn left, soon passing piped water from a woodland stream and continue along the road to **Jou** (1320m, **30min**). If you want water, fork left into Jou and pass two water points. Otherwise continue along the main road and, at the last house, fork right down steps, then fork right down a path. At a viewpoint near the bottom of the hill veer right onto a track which soon becomes a tarmac road. Turn left at a junction down to **La Guingueta d'Àneu** (940m, **30min**). The water point and seating area is slightly south of the Poldo Hotel. Next to Pont de Poldo there are nice grassy areas on the banks of La Noguera Pallaressa.

La Guingueta d'Àneu is a hamlet with a hotel, hostal and two campgrounds. Nou Camping also has cabins, a bar-restaurant and a small supermarket which stocks 'original' and 'easy-clic' camping gas. Camping Vall d'Àneu has minimal supplies and operates a taxi service. There are buses to Lleida and Barcelona.

FACILITIES ON STAGE 26

Camping La Mola: tel 973 624 024 www.campinglamola.com

Hotel Poldo: tel 973 626 080 www.hotelpoldo.com

Nou Camping: tel 973 626 261 www.noucamping.com

Camping Vall d'neu: tel 659 105 575
www.campingsdelleida.com/camping/vall-daneu/

Hotel Cases: tel 973 626 083 www.hotelcases.com

LA GUINGUETA D'ÀNEU –
PUIGCERDÀ

View from Pic de Comapedrosa (Stage 31)

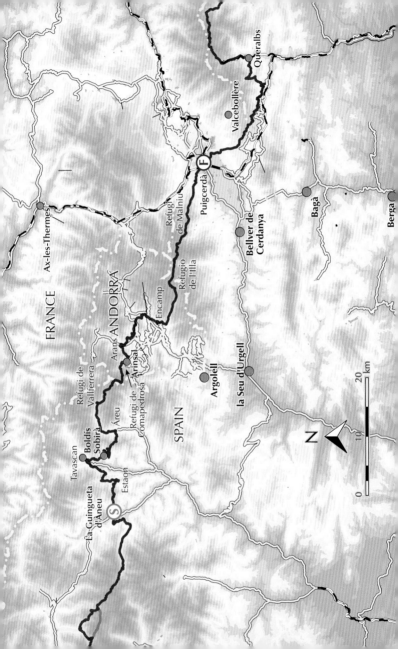

FRANCE

Ax-les-Thermes

ANDORRA

Refugi de
Vallferrera

Arans

Arinsal

Encamp

Refugi de
Malniu

Refugi de l'Illa

Puigcerdà

F

Valcebollère

Queralbs

Refugi de
Comapedrosa

Areu

Boldis
Sobirà

Tavascan

Estaon

S

La Guingueta
d'Aneu

SPAIN

Argolell

la Seu d'Urgell

Bellver de
Cerdanya

Bagà

Berga

N

0   10   20
km

Shepherd's hut below Refugi de l'Illa (Stage 34)

After crossing the highest section of the Pyrenean range, the first days of section four take you through relatively lower landscapes, with enchanting forests and charming Catalan villages. Some of these villages are abandoned, whereas others are lively with locals and tourists. Once in Andorra, there are again high passes and there is also the optional climb to Pic de Comapedrosa (2939m), which offers wide views. Andorra is crossed in three days, during which you pass through forested areas and finally follow the Madriu river all the way up to its lake source. Next you cross back into Spain and soon the large Cerdanya plateau comes into sight as you descend to Puigcerdà.

STAGE 27
La Guingueta d'Àneu to Estaon

Start	La Guingueta d'Àneu
Finish	Estaon
Time	5hr 35min
Distance	11.3km
Total ascent	1280m
Total descent	1000m
Difficulty	Although only a short route, it is tough because of the steepness of both ascent and descent.
High point	Coll de Montcaubo (2201m)

It is worth making an early start on this stage as the long steep ascent could be very tiring in the full heat of the day. Carry plenty of water when setting out from Dorve.

Cross the Pont de Poldo over the wide Noguera Pallaresa and turn right along the lake. Notice a well-preserved bunker window in the rockwall.

Seventeen **machine gun nests** were built around La Guingueta as part of Franco's Pyrenean defence line, but curiously these defences were constructed between 1947 and 1952, well after the end of the Spanish Civil War or World War II.

Fork left 200m up the road and soon fork left up a path to Dorve, which shortcuts the switchbacks on the road. Follow signposts and faint GR waymarks and walk into the hamlet of **Dorve** (1390m, **1hr 30min**). Dorve missed out on the building boom and most – if not all – of the houses are abandoned. Water point. The next water will probably be just before you reach Estaon. Go round the right-hand side of the church, after which the path veers back left.

Soon fork right, ignoring a left turn to Llavore and then a little further fork left and continue climbing on a well-waymarked path. There are good, dry campsites about 25min above Dorve. The path approaches the ridge north of Dorve, and then veers E before resuming the switchbacking climb to the **Collado de la Serra** on the ridge (1740m, **1hr 10min**).

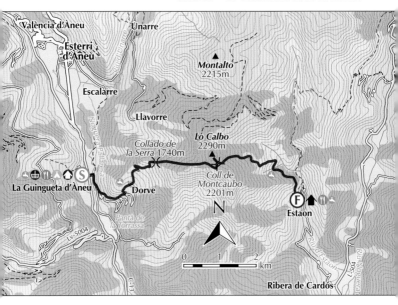

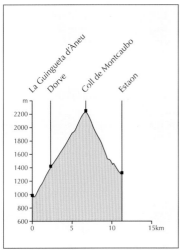

From the pass turn right (E) along a clear path, which takes you through the forest to a meadow (**50min**). Dry campsites. Continue through the meadow and back into the forest, heading up to the ridge (2110m, **25min**). Turn left up the ridge, but soon fork right and leave the ridge to traverse the south-western slopes of Calbo to reach its south-eastern ridge. Take care here, ignoring a path which continues along the ridge. The route swings left to reach the **Coll de Montcaubo** (2201m, **15min**). Good dry campsites. Lo Calbo (2290m), with its communication masts, is easily climbed from here (10min up, 5min down).

167

Evening view from Coll de Montcaubo

The path descends steeply NE from the col, gradually veering E then SE. Turn left at an old telegraph pole (**35min**) and right (S) at a junction (**20min**). This path soon crosses a woodland stream, the first reliable water since Dorve, although you may want to treat it before drinking. Pass a dilapidated house and follow an ancient path which drops gently down to **Estaon**. Follow the main street down to the water point and refuge in the centre of the hamlet (1240m, **30min**).

Refugi d'Estaon has full refuge facilities and is open all year.

FACILITIES ON STAGE 27
Refugi d'Estaon: tel 693 707 981 http://refugiestaon.com

STAGE 28

Estaon to Tavascan

Start	Estaon
Finish	Tavascan
Time	4hr 15min
Distance	12.8km
Total ascent	730m
Total descent	850m
Difficulty	Easy
High point	Coll de Jou (1830m)

This is an easy stage through an area with a rich agricultural past. Soon after leaving Estaon you re-enter the Parc Natural de l'Alt Pirineu.

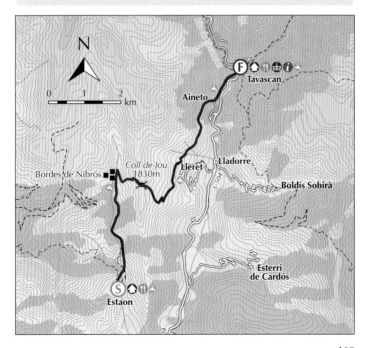

Deserted hamlet of Bordes de Nibrós

Go roughly E past Refugi d'Estaon to the end of the hamlet and turn left along an old path which gradually drops down to the Ríu d'Estaon. Cross it on a bridge to reach a dirt road and turn left. Soon fork right at a bridge and follow the old path up the right-hand bank of the river. Rejoin the road when it crosses again. The old path continues up the right-hand side of the stream to **Bordes de Nibrós** (1480m, **1hr 15min**). This deserted hamlet is largely derelict.

In a dry spell, your next water is likely to be at Lleret. Continue up the stream then turn sharp right at a signed junction. Pass a barn and switchback up the hill, going left of another barn, to reach the **Coll de Jou** (1830m, **1hr 5min**). Dry camping is possible at the col or at several places on the descent. Follow the path down from the col to a cattle trough then follow a poor track, initially SE, which switchbacks down to a bigger track. Turn left at this junction and contour before switchbacking down to **Lleret**. The water point with a seating area is at the top of the hamlet.

Continue down the tarmac access road to the first switchback and turn left up an old path. Soon cross a stream and shortly afterwards fork left and cross another stream before making a spectacular high-level traverse. Eventually this good path ends and you descend steeply down to **Aineto** (1220m, **1hr 40min**).

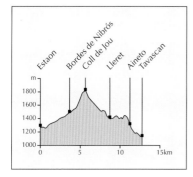

Water point on your left. Continue up a concrete ramp between the houses, keep straight on until the end of the hamlet and then turn left down another old path which takes you to **Tavascan**. Keep straight on past a water point and over the ancient bridge, then turn right to the information office on the main road (1120m, **15min**). All the tourist facilities in Tavascan are to your right.

For such a small village, Tavascan has good facilities for tourists, including a small food shop. Casa Feliu has a bar-restaurant and accommodation. Hotel Llacs de Cardós offers an early breakfast and discounts to GR11 hikers. Hotel Estanys Blaus is the upmarket part of the Llacs de Cardós organisation with the same contact details. The hotel owns the small outdoor store opposite the hotel, which sells 'easy-clic' and 'Coleman-style' camping gas. If the food shop or the outdoor store is closed when you are passing through ask at the Llacs de Cardós hotel and they will find someone to open them for you!

FACILITIES ON STAGE 28

Casa Rural Feliu: tel 973 623 163

Hotel Llacs de Cardós: tel 973 623 178 www.hotelllacsdecardos.com

Marxant Hotel: tel 973 623 151 www.hotelmarxant.com

Tavascan Information Office: tel 973 623 079 www.tavascan.net

STAGE 29
Tavascan to Àreu

Start	Tavascan
Finish	Àreu
Time	6hr 30min
Distance	16.7km
Total ascent	1245m
Total descent	1095m
Difficulty	Easy
High point	Coll de Tudela (2243m)

This is a final easy section in the foothills before returning to the alpine mountains.

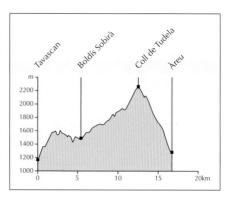

Cross the wooden bridge by the information office and follow a path which climbs steeply until you come to a signed junction by some ruined stone huts (1530m, **1hr 20min**). Turn right (take care not to end up on the path which forks left as there is a shortcut to that path a little before the junction), continuing S along an old path. Navigate two easy parts with chains and cross several woodland streams before reaching **Boldís Sobirà** (1510m, **1hr 10min**). There are several water points in Boldís Sobirà, but the one on the right as you exit the hamlet is probably the best quality one.

Keep going in the same direction and leave along a signed track, which veers E to cross a pair of streams before veering south-west and passing the Font de la Plana. The track switchbacks left when it reaches the **Roc Bataller ridge** (1710m) and right (1900m) to return to the ridge (**1hr 30min**). Head up the ridge through

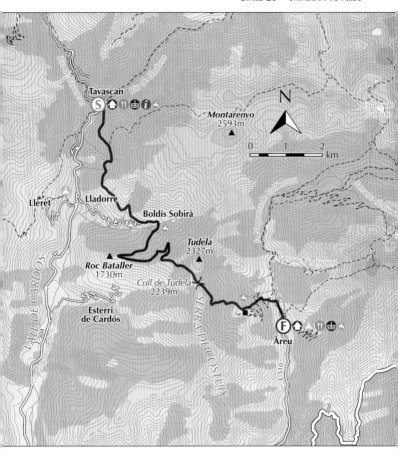

brush and almost immediately turn left and then right along a path. Dry camping is possible here. The path climbs through thick and more open forest to reach a flat area which leads to **Coll de Tudela** (2239m, **1hr 5min**). Dry camping. Follow a clear path, initially SE, as it switchbacks down to Bordes de Costuix in meadows (**45min**). Camping possible. Descend right of a building and turn right after about 30m onto a track which you follow past a water point in a gully. Immediately afterwards the GR11 forks left down a path. This path shortcuts many switchbacks

A rare technical bit on the climb from Tavascan to Bordís Sobirà

on the track and can be followed all the way down to the road at the northern end of **Àreu**. Water point on the right at the junction. If you don't want Àreu you can turn left here and start Stage 30. Otherwise turn right to the centre of Àreu (1270m, **40min**).

Àreu has a small shop, hotel, and several casas rurales offering accommodation. If the shop is shut ask at the hotel for it to be opened. Camping Pica d'Estats, which also has a bar-restaurant and cabins, is open from April to October.

FACILITIES ON STAGE 29

Hotel Vallferrera: tel 973 624 343 www.hotelvallferrera.com

Casa Besolí: tel 973 624 415 www.casabesoli.es

Camping Pica d'Estats: tel 973 624 347 www.picadestats.com

STAGE 30
Àreu to Refugi de Vallferrera

Start	Àreu
Finish	Refugi de Vallferrera
Time	3hr 20min
Distance	10km
Total ascent	740m
Total descent	90m
Difficulty	Easy
High point	Refugi de Vallferrera (1920m)

This short walk up the Vall Ferrera is popular with tourists. It sets you up for the high-level crossing into Andorra the next day. If you are camping or are happy to use an unmanned refuge, you will probably want to continue further up the valley to Refugi de Baiau, 3hr further on.

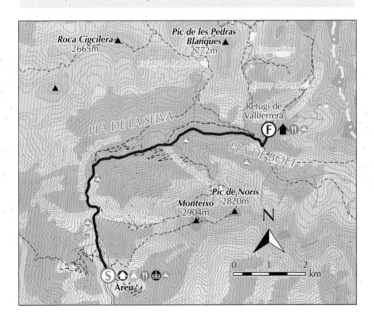

Head up the road that soon becomes a dirt road, which may be busy with tourist cars. Fork right across **La Noguera de Vallferrera** (**45min**) and 5min later fork right up an old path which climbs steadily. When you reach a meadow with some barns (**45min**), the path goes between walls to the right of the meadow to reach a larger track. Turn left along this to reach the dirt road at a signed junction. Turn right and immediately left. At the next meeting with the dirt road, turn left

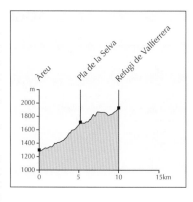

along it and then fork left at the Pla de la Selva, which has a picnic site (1695m, **20min**). A sign here reminds you that you are only allowed to camp above 2000m and between 20:00 and 8:00.

A few minutes later fork right on a path which joins a track as it contours through the forest high above the river. Water point at 1860m. Eventually fork right up a path (**50min**) and follow this to the large car park at La Molinassa

The trail near Pla de la Selva

(**20min**). Keep straight on at the top of the car park, shortcutting the last switch-back on the track, then follow the track. Five minutes later there is a left turn across a bridge (**1840m**) signed to the Refugi de Vallferrera.

The GR11 continues up the Vall Ferrera and doesn't visit the refuge. If you don't need the refuge continue along the track and start Stage 31. Otherwise turn left and follow the path to the **Refugi de Vallferrera** (1920m, **20min**).

Refugi de Vallferrera offers a full refuge service. Open June to October.

FACILITIES ON STAGE 30

Refugi de Vallferrera: tel 973 624 378 (12:00–16:00) www.feec.cat

STAGE 31
Refugi de Vallferrera to Refugi de Comapedrosa

Start	Refugi de Vallferrera
Finish	Refugi de Comapedrosa
Time	5hr 20min
Distance	10.4km
Total ascent	1000m
Total descent	660m
Difficulty	There is a lot of boulderfield and some scree on the crossing of a high alpine pass. The route would be a serious undertaking in bad weather or early in the season when there may be snow. The ascent in snow should only be attempted by properly equipped, experienced mountaineers. Start early in the morning so you cross the high point before any possible afternoon thunderstorms.
High point	Portella de Baiau (2757m)

This stage is a classic High Pyrenees route. It is a demanding crossing of the Portella de Baiau from Spain into Andorra. It would be possible to continue down to the ski resort of Arinsal (see Stage 32) for full tourist facilities.

Return to the main track in the Vall Ferrera. The GR11 continues along the track
to reach the Pla de Boet (1850m, **10min**). Picnic site, water point. There is good
camping with water at regular intervals all the way to the Refugi de Baiau.

> The **Vall Ferrera**, like many valleys on the border between France and Spain,
> has seen a lot of military action, with border raids a common occurrence
> in the past. In 1597 a French army of 2000 Lutherans crossed the Port de
> Boet and sacked the villages of Vall Ferrera in a massacre that was out of
> proportion with normal raids. The Republican Pyrenees Battalion was based
> here during the Spanish Civil War and they prepared a route over the snow-
> covered Port de Boet to allow Republican soldiers and civilians to escape to
> France after defeat by the Fascist army of Franco.

The GR11 stays on the track to the right of the Pla de Boet. The waymarking isn't very good ahead but look out for cairns when waymarks are missing. Leave the track at a switchback, keeping straight. Cross several wooden
bridges to arrive at the meadows of the Pla d'Arcalis (2000m, **35min**). At a
junction, stay right of the stream as you pass through a semi-wooded area of

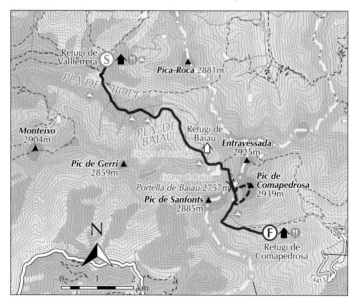

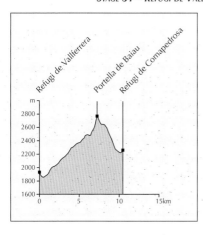

the meadow, heading roughly SE and gradually veering E, to reach a wet grassy area, Pla de Baiau (2130m, **40min**). The path crosses a stream here and veers round the left-hand side of the rocky ridge ahead and climbs easily, veering SSE up its grassy north-eastern flank to reach the **Estanys d'Ascorbes** (2360m, **55min**). The path continues roughly SE to the Estany de Baiau (lower lake of two) from where you climb to the **Refugi de Baiau** (2517m, **40min**) on the rocky knoll on your left.

The well-maintained, purpose-built Refugi de Baiau has nine bunks.

From the hut go E down a gully and veer left across rock before you descend to the northern end of **Estany de Baiau** (upper lake). Last campsites on the ascent. Head along the shore, cross a boulderfield, then follow the path which heads away from the lake. At the top of a grassy slope keep straight on across a little valley, veering to the right to follow a route through boulderfields and scree. The going is rather easy until you get to the final steeper slopes, just below the col. Find the most stable underground in a wide corridor and reach the **Portella de Baiau** (2757m, **1hr 20min**), where you enter Andorra. Camping laws are the same as in Spain and fires are not permitted.

Soon after you start descending, a path on your left goes up to **Pic de Comapedrosa** (2939m, 30min up, 45min down to join the GR11 again near Estany Negre). This is a great opportunity to enjoy the wide views this high mountain offers. After summiting, follow yellow marks S and then SW down the ridge and join the GR11 again in between Estany Negre and Estany de Comapedrosa.

Descend easily SSE, soon veering right past Estany Negre and Estany de Comapedrosa. Cross the outlet of the lower lake and follow the path down the right-hand side of the valley into the Coma Pedrosa, a classic hanging valley. This valley provides the only good wild camping during the descent. Reach a signed path junction (**50min**) where you fork right to the **Refugi de Comapedrosa** on a shelf just above the valley floor (2260m, **10min**).

View just below Pic de Comapedrosa

Refugi de Comapedrosa is a modern manned refuge with full refuge facilities.
It is open from June until the end of September.

FACILITIES ON STAGE 31

Refugi de Comapedrosa: tel (+376) 327 995
https://refugicomapedrosa.ad

STAGE 32

Refugi de Comapedrosa to Arans

Start	Refugi de Comapedrosa
Finish	Arans
Time	4hr
Distance	9.7km
Total ascent	535m
Total descent	1435m
Difficulty	Easy
High points	Refugi de Comapedrosa (2260m), Coll de les Cases (1958m)

An easy descent down to the ski resort Arinsal is followed by a steep crossing of the south ridge of Pic de Percanela at the Coll de les Cases. It would be possible to continue into Stage 33 and stay overnight at Ordino.

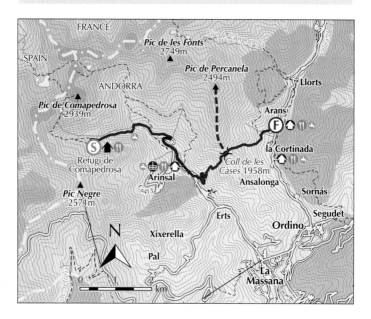

Go down NW from the refuge and turn right at the junction to rejoin the GR11. Continue down the right-hand side of the Riu de Pedrosa, eventually crossing it and the Riu d'Areny on bridges and soon reaching a track at the boundary of the natural park (**55min**).

Almost immediately fork right and follow the track down to the avalanche wall which crosses the valley. The track becomes a tarmac road as it reaches buildings and soon after crosses the river. Turn left through the short road tunnel under the avalanche wall to arrive at the top of **Arinsal** (**20min**). Fork left down the road, passing several water points to the main facilities in the ski resort, which are about 1km down the road. Continue down the main street until a mini-roundabout just after the second supermarket and turn left up a road signed 'El Mas de Ribafeta'. Follow the road as it switchbacks up the hill until,

Camping at Coll de les Cases (photo: Brian Johnson)

at the top, a footpath 'Camí del Coll de la Cases' goes off left at a bend (**30min**). Follow this path steeply up to the **Coll de les Cases** (1954m, **1hr 25min**). Good dry campsites. There is a waymarked path left from here to Pic de Percanela (2494m).

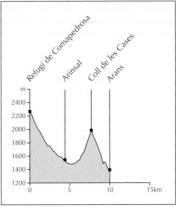

Arinsal is a ski resort which seems to stay fully open in the summer. There are numerous hotels, bars and restaurants to choose between, as well as two supermarkets and other shops. Esports St Moritz stocks 'Coleman-style' camping gas.

Follow the well-marked path steeply downhill, ignoring a few side turns. Turn left as you approach the bottom of the hill, cross a stream (**35min**) and climb a little above meadows before descending again and completing the descent on a track to reach a tarmac road. Turn right and switchback down, following waymarked shortcuts. Pass a water point and reach the centre of **Arans** on the main road (1360m, **15min**).

Arans is a small hamlet with two hotels and three bar-restaurants, but no shop.

FACILITIES ON STAGE 32

Hotel Antic: tel (+376) 850 988 www.hotelantic.com

Aparthotel La Tulipa: tel 376 835 086 www.pierreetvacances.com

STAGE 33

Arans to Encamp

Start	Arans
Finish	Encamp
Time	6hr
Distance	14.9km
Total ascent	1085m
Total descent	1175m
Difficulty	Easy
High point	Coll d'Ordino (1983m)

The walk described in Stage 32 from Arinsal to Arans and its continuation here in Stage 33 manage to find a quiet route avoiding the noise, congestion and supermarkets of Andorra's main towns.

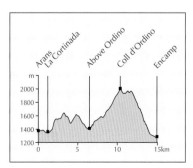

Cross the main road and go down the road opposite the Restaurant La Tulipa to cross the river. Then turn right along a track, signed to La Cortinada, which becomes a path before reaching a tarmac road. Cross the bridge here and turn left down the main road to reach **La Cortinada**. If you want the centre of the hamlet keep on down the road.

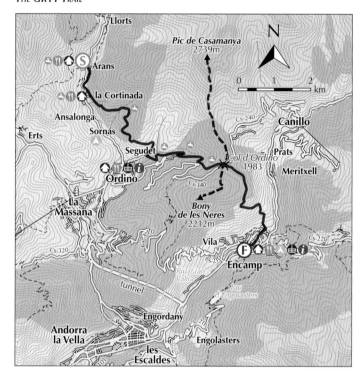

La Cortinada is a hamlet with several hotels and bar-restaurants, but no shop.

The GR11 goes left across a bridge. Water point on the left. Continue along an old, cobbled street before reaching the next bridge and take the road left of a golf course. Water point on the left. The road soon becomes a track, then a path. Fork left, signed to Les Planes de Sornas, and climb steeply with switchbacks until you reach a ridge (**1hr**). There are dry camping possibilities here or ahead. Contour above some meadows with barns and keep straight on at a junction, following a sign to Ordino. In this section there are lots of side paths, but you follow the waymarked main path. Soon cross a stream and start climbing again before a considerable descent. Then climb to and up another ridge (**1hr 20min**). Then descend steeply to a track and turn right, signed to Ordino. Descend switchbacks to a track junction at a stream. Turn right and 100m later turn sharp left across the

Font de la Navina (photo: Brian Johnson)

stream and follow a path signed to Coll d'Ordino (**25min**). Go straight on here if you need Ordino, which is about 10min away.

> Ordino is a tourist village with a tourist information office, lots of hotels, a small range of shops and a campground.

You now follow the stream, crossing it several times and then veer right up a tributary to reach a picnic area (**45min**). Turn right down the track and then fork left up a smaller track. This track veers left before switchbacking right, forking left and left again along a path which leads to a second picnic site at the Font de la Navina (**40min**). Water point. Fork left up a path immediately above the picnic area and join a track which becomes a path to reach the road and car park at the **Coll d'Ordino** (1983m, **40min**).

> **Bony de les Neres** (2212m) to the south-west is an easy walk, but unfortunately the summit is dominated by a communications complex (30min up, 20min down). **Pic de Casamanya** (2739m) to the north is a much more worthwhile climb. There is a good path all the way to the summit (1hr 40min up, 55min down).

Cross the road and follow a grass path to an orientation table and signpost. Follow signs, roughly SE, to Encamp les Bons. Take care, as there are other paths from the orientation table. Ignore a turn to Ríu d'Urina Racons as you cross grassland. Excellent dry campsites. Take care to follow the waymarks, as there are several other paths in the area. Once you are descending through the woods go left at a signed junction (**20min**) and then cross a small stream several times lower down the descent. Near the bottom you pass a ruined castle and the old chapel just above the town of **Encamp** (1270m, **40min**).

> **Torre de los Moros** (tower of the Moors) is the remains of a larger fort which would have dominated the area in medieval days. The Lombard Romanesque Church of Sant Romà de les Bons was consecrated in 1164.

Continue down to a tarmac road, Carrer de St Romà. Water point. Follow this road as it switchbacks down to and across the Pont de les Bons. Veer right (WSW) down the Avinguda de Rouillac to reach a main road. Cross the main road and go down some steps, cw the first left on Plaça del Consell to arrive at the tourist information office (**10min**). Nearby there are shops, hotels and bar-restaurants.

> Encamp is a town with all facilities for tourists, such as hotels, restaurants, supermarkets and a campground. Tècnic Esports, to the south-east of the town, is a good outdoor store which stocks all types of camping gas. There is a bus link to Barcelona and Barcelona Airport. Camping Internacional has cabins and a bar-restaurant.

FACILITIES ON STAGE 33

Ordino Tourist Office: tel (+376) 878 173 www.ordino.ad

Encamp Tourist Office: tel (+376) 731 000 www.encamp.ad

Camping Internacional: tel (+376) 831 609

STAGE 34
Encamp to Refugio de l'Illa

Start	Encamp
Finish	Refugio de l'Illa
Time	5hr 45min
Distance	15.8km
Total ascent	1370m
Total descent	155m
Difficulty	Easy
High points	Coll Jovell (1779m), Refugio de l'Illa (2485m)

The two-day crossing back into Catalonia is the final alpine section of the GR11. This stage ends at the modern Refugio de l'Illa. On the way there is a wide choice of charming and private accommodation in one of the many unstaffed huts.

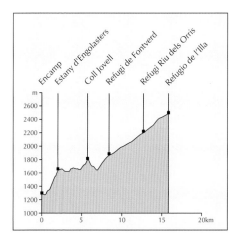

Go down the road to the left of the tourist office and fork left up Carrer de Sant Miquel. Turn right at the end of the road and 30m further fork left up Carrer de l'Arena. Veer slightly right across a roundabout and continue on Carrer de l'Arena. After 150m, turn left at a junction and climb to a roundabout. Cross and climb steps on the other side, signed to Llac d'Engolasters, and follow an old path in between hedges. Keep straight on at a junction by an electricity pylon and follow signs left at the next pylon. Follow GR markings as you climb, ignoring a number of side turns until you pass a building (**1hr**). Immediately after this building there are dry campsites on a flat semi-wooded area on your right. Continue climbing to reach the eastern end of **Estany d'Engolasters**, where there are two bar-restaurants and toilets (1616m, **20min**).

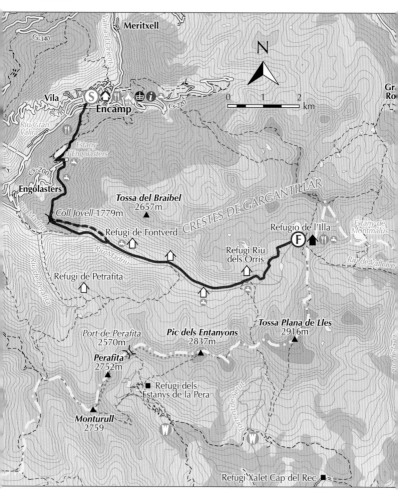

Follow the track along the southern shore of the reservoir, forking left up a tarmac road at the dam, and follow this road to the second switchback, where there is a car park and information office. Head roughly SW past the information office along a track signed 'Camé dels Matxos'. This track contours and soon passes the Font de les Ordigues. Water. Fork right and pass through a short tunnel, pass a viewpoint and reach the Font de les Molleres. Water. This track ends at a picnic site with an open shelter at Font dels Corralets (**35min**). The water point here may be dry. Continue along the path, ignoring a couple of side turns, as it climbs gently to **Coll Jovell** where there is a picnic table (1779m, **25min**). It is recommended that you follow the more scenic higher-level traverse, also signed to Refugi de Fontverd and waymarked with yellow dots, rejoining the GR11 in 55 minutes. The GR11 continues down a good path which gradually takes you down to Riu Madriu. At the bottom pass a rough hut, which could serve as an emergency shelter, just before a signed junction where the higher route comes in (1638m). The GR11 continues NE and climbs steadily, ignoring several side turns. Pass an old hut before arriving at the **Refugi de Fontverd** (eight places in metal bunk beds, **1hr 5min**).

This is a modern, well-maintained unmanned refuge with piped water outside. This is where you will find the first good campsites in the valley. There are frequent excellent campsites throughout the remainder of the section.

Early morning at Riu Madriu

Continue climbing past a basic cabin (six places on a wooden floor) and immediately afterwards fork left, staying left of the main stream (**25min**). Ignore a log bridge on the right (**45min**) which leads to a charming, small cabin across the stream. Reach a beautiful flat area, Pla de l'Ingla, and continue to the **Refugi Riu dels Orris** (six places in metal bunk beds, 2230m, **15min**). Soon after this pass a farmer's hut, after which the path veers left away from the stream. You pass another small hut as the path winds between granite knolls. Turn right at a junction, pass a tarn, cross a stream and eventually reach the **Refugio de l'Illa** (2485m, **55min**). This refuge, with full refuge facilities, was opened in 2017. Piped water outside. See Stage 35 if you want to climb a peak from the refuge.

FACILITIES ON STAGE 34

Refugio de l'Illa: tel (+376) 775 776 www.refugidelilla.ad

STAGE 35
Refugio de l'Illa to Refugi de Malniu

Start	Refugio de l'Illa
Finish	Refugi de Malniu
Time	5hr 35min
Distance	14.3km
Total ascent	780m
Total descent	1125m
Difficulty	There is some rough going. Although the route is well waymarked, care would be needed with navigation in poor visibility.
High points	Coll de Vall Civera (2550m), Portella d'Engorgs (2680m)

A beautiful hike through landscapes dotted with lakes. You will often be following streams, so water isn't a problem. There are also plenty of camping opportunities along the route.

Follow the path to the right end of the dam, just above the refuge, and continue in the same direction to a signpost above the reservoir.

Near Portella d'Engorgs

Pic dels Pessons (2864m) to the north is an easy peak from here. Follow the GR7 until it contours left of the summit then head up the ridge to the summit (55min up, 35min down). Tossa Plana de Lles (2916m), to the south, is another easy peak.

The GR7 forks left and the GR11 right, to reach the grassy **Coll de Vall Civera** (2550m, **15min**). This is where you leave Andorra and re-enter Catalonia. Follow the well-marked path steeply down the other side to the valley floor and then down the left-hand bank of the Riu de Vallcivera to reach the **Cabana dels Esparvers** (small and low, 3 places on a wooden floor) in a large meadow as you approach the bottom of the valley (2068m, **1hr 5min**).

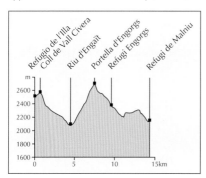

Ascend a small rise E, then descend slightly left to a signpost and turn right (E) across the Riu d'Engaït. Follow the well-waymarked route up lightly wooded pasture. Cross a small stream (**35min**). Good camping and water. Continue climbing to reach the floor of a small corrie (**45min**), climb steeply out of it and then veer left up a grassy hillside to the broad **Portella d'Engorgs** (2680m, **40min**).

191

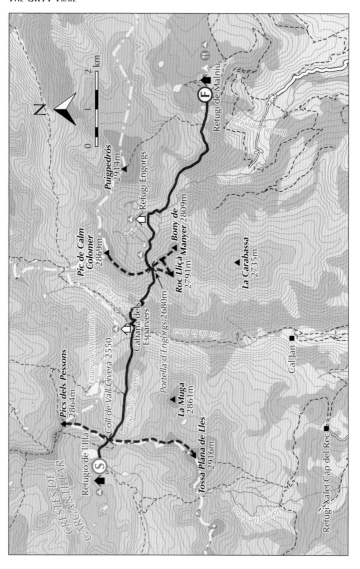

View to the Cerdanya plateau

You could climb **Pic de Calm Colomer** (2869m) to the north from here. Easy scrambling is required on the shattered rocky ridge, but all the difficulties can be avoided by staying below the ridge on the south-east face (45min up, 30min down). If you want easier summits you could climb Roc Lliçà (2791m) to the SSW of the col and then traverse Bony de Manyer Nord (2806m) en route to Bony de Manyer (2809m). The round trip is about 1hr. There is a curious 'border' stone on the summit of Bony de Manyer inscribed with the Roman 'XV'.

Stick to the well-marked path down a short steep descent to reach Estany de la Portella, then veer right over boulderfield to further lakes, the Estanys dels Minyons. You need to keep a close eye on the cairns and waymarks in mist as the path is very indistinct. Continue roughly E to the **Refugi Engorgs** (also named Refugi J Folch I Girona), a cosy unmanned hut (12 places, 2380m, **35min**).

Head SSE from the hut, cross the stream and head up a slight rise on the other side. The path doesn't head up the ridge but follows a line above the stream. Follow it on a tortuous traverse of the steep southern slopes of Puigpedrós (2914m) and climb steadily to reach a grassy ridge (2320m, **1hr 15min**). Catch the amazing views to the Cerdanya plateau ahead of you as you follow the path down to the **Refugi de Malniu** (2138m, **25min**), situated beside a small lake.

The popular Refugi de Malniu provides a full refuge service. There is also a car park, toilet block with showers, picnic area, water point, basic campground (small fee, no shade) and permanent orienteering course. Open mid June to mid September and some weekends outside this period.

FACILITIES ON STAGE 35

Refugi de Malniu: tel 616 855 535 www.refugimalniu.com

STAGE 36
Refugi de Malniu to Puigcerdà

Start	Refugi de Malniu
Finish	Puigcerdà
Time	3hr 10min
Distance	14.2km
Total ascent	95m
Total descent	1030m
Difficulty	Easy
High point	North slope of Planell de l'Agulla (2217m)

This is an easy downhill section to reach the high plateau around Puigcerdà.

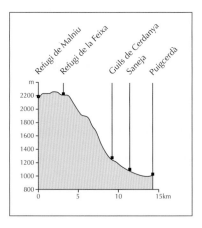

Cross the footbridge east of the refuge and then turn left along a path. The GR11 waymarking is unclear in the start. First climb gently following the yellow marks of local path 119 and then those of path 120. The GR11 then veers right, gradually climbing the gentle ridge to reach a large grassy area (**30min**) with a dirt road visible ahead. Veer left alongside the edge of the grassy area, now following local path 139, turning left along the dirt road to reach a signpost at the beginning of another large grassy area, the Pla de la Feixa (**10min**). Cows and horses roam free here, so camping is not advised. A much better option is the staffed **Refugi de la Feixa** (2160m), 200m ahead. There is a water point 100m beyond the refuge.

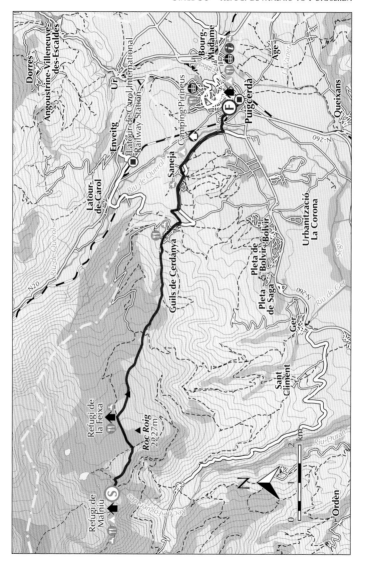

Early morning at Refugi de la Feixa

Refugi de la Feixa (12 places, open from June to mid September and all year round on weekends) is a cabana which has been converted into a small refuge. It's a one-of-a-kind small, staffed refuge offering local food (traditional mountain food and vegetarian/vegan food) and accommodation in a cosy dormitory. If you are just passing you can also buy food and drinks.

To follow the GR11, turn diagonally right across Pla de la Feixa, veering slightly right (SE), then left (E) to pick up a faint grassy track which takes you to the eastern top of Roc Roig (2170m, **10min**). It is now downhill all the way to Puigcerdà. Descend easily on pasture through woodland to a dirt road. Keep straight on across this road, now following local path 200, go down the ridge and reach a signpost in a grassy area (**45min**). This is the last camping opportunity on the descent.

Continue down the now stonier ridge to reach a track just above the village **Guils de Cerdanya**. Follow the track which soon becomes a tarmac road and go into the village. Veer left down to a junction and turn right. The Font de la Canal is on your left. Fork left, passing another water point, and descend to a junction.

Early morning light on the way down to Puigcerdà

Continue SE across a bridge over Torrent de Llosers. The GR11 now reaches a main road, GIV-4035 (**30min**). Follow this road shortly, then turn left up a track and turn right at a junction to return to the main road. Turn left at the road, then turn left again further on and go into the village of **Saneja**. Water point on the left. Keep straight on to reach the church (1220m, **35min**), then veer right back to the main road and turn left.

Camping Pirineus also has cabins, a bar-restaurant and a shop which stocks 'original' and 'Coleman-style' camping gas.

Pass Camping Pirineus and continue to a junction in St Martí d'Aravó (**20min**). Turn left, cross the bridge and enter **Puigcerdà**. Follow the road right to a roundabout. Water point on the left. Go across the railway bridge to a junction and turn right. The GR11 turns left at Carrer del Pont (continue straight on here to reach the Puigcerdà railway station) and then right onto Avinguda dels Pireneus (1204m, **10min**).

Puigcerdà is a town with all facilities, most of which are at the top of the hill. Butano Cerdánya, in Carrer Font d'en Lleres, stocks all types of camping gas. There are many hotels and hostals – the three closest to the station are listed. There are rail links to Barcelona, Toulouse and Perpignan from Puigcerdà.

FACILITIES ON STAGE 36

Camping Pirineus: tel 972 881 062 www.stel.es

Hostal l'Estació: tel 972 880 350 www.hostalestaciopuigcerda.com

Hotel Tèrminus: tel 972 880 212 www.hotelterminus.net

Hotel Puigcerdà: tel 972 882 181 www.hotelpuigcerda.cat

Puigcerdà Tourist Office: tel 972 880 542 www.puigcerdaturisme.cat

PUIGCERDÀ – CAP DE CREUS

Crossing a fence near Coll de Lliens (Stage 40)

This final section starts with two days of fast, easy hiking that bring you to the Núria monastery. Above Núria the GR11 reaches its highest point as you hike on the border crest. You then leave the high mountains behind and enter forested hills. Dry and hot conditions are to be expected in this part of the Pyrenees and the shade found in the forests is often more than welcome. Again, there are plenty of Catalan villages along the trail, allowing for frequent resupply. After crossing the border town of La Jonquera, you are mainly hiking through garrigue landscapes with cork oaks and aromatic shrubs. Several small rivers bring life into this otherwise dry landscape. A day before the end of the trail you reach the Mediterranean Sea at Llança. On the final day the GR11 takes you up into the hills again and then goes down to the fishing harbour and tourist center of El Port de la Selva. Beyond El Port de la Selva you enter the Cap de Creus Natural Park, where beautiful, quiet paths lead you to the Cap de Creus lighthouse and the trail end beyond, at the easternmost point of the Spanish mainland, where the Pyrenees plunge into the Mediterranean Sea.

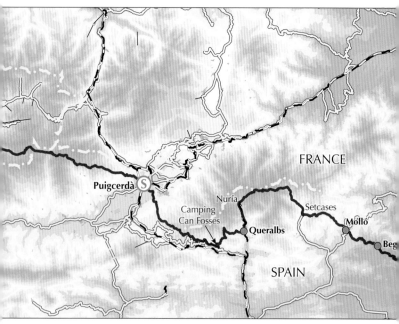

View to Queralbs from near Font dels Plaus (Stage 38)

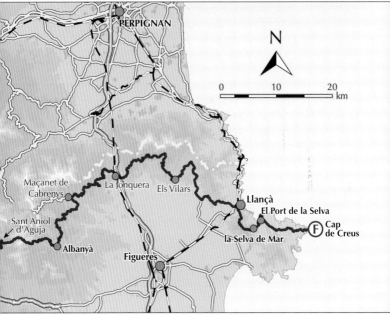

STAGE 37

Puigcerdà to Camping Can Fosses

Start	Puigcerdà
Finish	Camping Can Fosses
Time	6hr 50min
Distance	27.1km
Total ascent	1055m
Total descent	1000m
Difficulty	Easy and fast walking
High points	Coll de Marcer (1980m), Coll de la Creu de Meians (2000m)

The 'alpine' mountains are now behind you and the next three days are through the high but gentler mountains which form the border between Spain and France. You may prefer to continue to Refugi Corral Blanc, a steep climb into Stage 38.

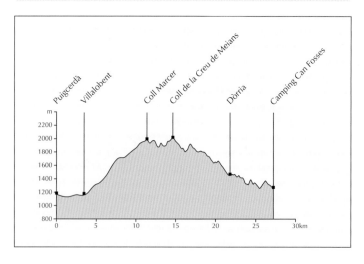

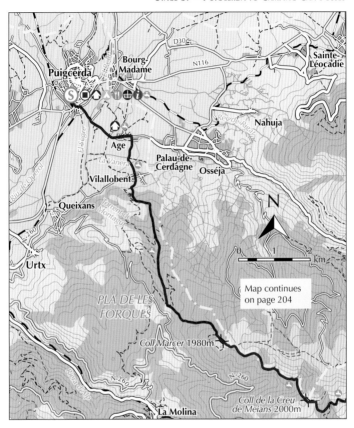

Walk SW on Avinguda dels Pirineus, go straight on at a roundabout and straight on again at a junction where the name changes to Carretera de Vilallobent. Cross the N-152 and go to the end of Camí d'Age where you turn left and immediately right to continue down the road signed to Age and Vilallobent. Don't get confused by GR4 waymarks. Soon cross a bridge over El Segre and walk into **Age** (**25min**). Water point left from the main square, Plaça Major.

Age has a 'turisme rural' called Cal Marrufès.

Coll de la Creu de Meians

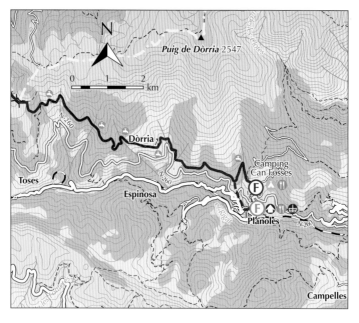

GR11 waymarks seem to be absent in Age, but the route is easy to follow: after walking 500m E through the village, the road veers right (signed for Vilallobent) as you leave the hamlet. Keep straight on (S), cross a bridge over La Vanera and walk into **Vilallobent** (1170m, **20min**). Water point in the park on the right. About 150m after reaching the first house, continue S up a concrete track (Camí Torre de Roset) which soon turns to gravel. As this gravel track veers right, the GR11 forks left up a rough track (signpost). This shortcut eventually returns to the better track (**20min**). Turn left and follow a wide track, ignoring junctions, until you eventually fork right up a path (**1hr**) to cross the Torrent de Montagut (1645m), which may be dry – if running, it would need treating before drinking.

> There are good, dry campsites as you follow the stream up, and plenty of campsites all the way to the Torrent del Pla de les Salines.

You reach some tracks on the ridge at the Pla de les Forques (1719m, **15min**). Turn left (SE) along the second of these tracks and continue up to a sharp right-hand bend (**30min**). Leave the track, turning left up a path next to a probably dried-up stream to reach a signpost on the ridge (**15min**) just below Border Stone 500 at the **Coll Marcer** (1946m).

Go down SE from the col and soon join a track which takes you past a succession of border stones, starting with Stone 501, to a stream by Border Stone 501-VI (**25min**). Climb gently to Border Stone 502 on a grassy ridge at **Coll de la Creu de Meians** (2000m, **25min**).

Head ESE from the metal cross at the pass (ignoring tracks going left and right) and then SSE down a wet area to reach a track (**10min**). Turn left along the track to reach a junction. The GR11 leaves the track for some distance (a little before Torrent de Sant Salvador crosses it) and continues a little lower, parallel to the track. But this GR11 path is overgrown, so it is recommended that you continue on the track, forking right shortly before the GR11 joins the track again (**40min**). Descend along the track, taking two shortcuts as the track starts switchbacking down to the Torrent del Pla de les Salines. Good camping.

Fork right and reach **Dòrria** (**50min**). The GR11 does not enter the village but continues along a concrete track and switchbacks down to join a tarmac road at the lower end of Dòrria.

It is recommended to leave the GR11 by turning right to go down into Dòrria. Rejoin the GR11 at the north-east end (at the start of the tarmac road mentioned above) of this small, authentic village. There is a water point and seating area beside the church.

Go down shortly S on the tarmac road and then turn sharp left (N) down a track and soon turn right down a path immediately before a stream. The path stays roughly level as it traverses above the road to reach an open ridge (**25min**). The path has become a track by the time you reach a signpost at Serrat de Mestre (1272m, **30min**). If you want to go to Planoles turn right down the concrete track.

> Planoles is a large village focused on tourism. It has a variety of accommodation, two very small shops, a bakery and bar-restaurants.

The GR11 goes left on a track, crossing a stream and turning right. Reach a signpost at Can Fosses (1300m, **15min**) and turn right to arrive at **Camping Can Fosses** (1260m, **5min**).

> Camping Can Fosses also has cabins and a bar.

FACILITIES ON STAGE 37

Cal Marrufès: tel 972 141 174 www.calmarrufes.cat

Can Gasparó: tel 722 220 940 www.hotelcangasparo.com

Camping Can Fosses: tel 972 736 065 www.canfosses.com

Cal Sadurni: tel 972 736 135

STAGE 38

Camping Can Fosses to Núria

Start	Camping Can Fosses
Finish	Núria
Time	6hr 25min
Distance	18.2km
Total ascent	1475m
Total descent	770m
Difficulty	Easy. Adequate waymarking to Queralbs, after which Núria is well signed.
High points	Collet de les Barraques (1890m), Creu d'en Riba (1983m)

This stage takes you up the spectacular Gorges de Núria. You could break the section as there is accommodation at Refugi Corral Blanc and Queralbs en route. It is possible to shortcut along the GR11.8, avoiding the descent to Queralbs, but this means missing out on the ascent of the Gorges de Núria. Camping is not permitted in the 'Queralbs Municipal Area' which includes the surroundings of Núria. In Núria itself there is a campground.

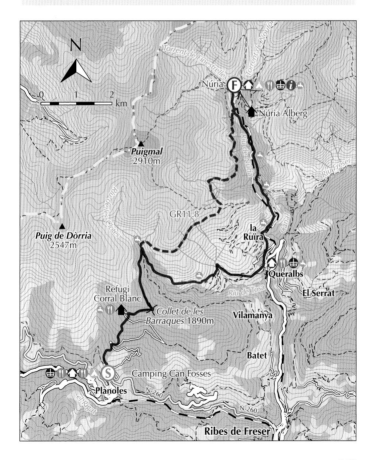

From Camping Can Fosses, return up the track, fork right and follow a path steeply uphill. Cross a track and then a tarmac road. Soon arrive at the same road again, turn right along it and leave it again at a bend, turning left onto a path. This steep path climbs easily through pleasant woodland. Fork left and further cross a track and then cross the road to reach a large picnic site (1825m, **1hr 25min**). The

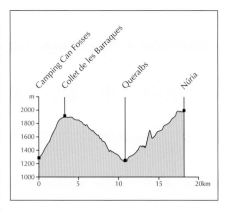

lower water point may be dry, but the higher one should be flowing. The manned **Refugi Corral Blanc** is just to the left of the picnic site.

> Refugi Corral Blanc is a cosy refuge which has full refuge facilities and is open from mid June to mid September, and at weekends outside this period.

Continue up through the picnic area to the road and turn right along it to the car park at the roadhead at **Collet de les Barraques** (1884m, **15min**). Turn left (NW) along a track and follow it until you reach a grassy area, Pla dels Ventolanesos, which has the best dry campsites in this section. Fork right along a very faint waymarked path which becomes better defined as it gradually descends through the forest to the Torrent de l'Estremera (1800m, **30min**). Cross the stream. Font de l'Home Mort is 100m upstream and has the best water here. You will find some small streams and possible campsites between Torrent de l'Estremera and Queralbs, but the quality of both may depend on the latest cow activity. There are two ways to continue from here to Núria.

FACILITIES ON STAGE 38

Refugi Corral Blanc: tel 626 274 395 www.corral-blanc.com

Hostal Les Roquetes: tel 972 727 369

Hotel Vall de Núria: tel 972 732 000 www.hotelvalldenuria.cat

Hostal Núria (Alberg Pic de l'Àliga): tel 972 732 048

Núria Tourist Office: tel 972 732 020 www.valldenuria.cat

Alternative route via GR11.8

The GR11.8 variant goes left just after crossing the footbridge over Torrent de l'Estremera. A sign on a rock shows the right direction. It takes a direct route to Núria following a combination of yellow and white, yellow, red and GR waymarks. Head NNE and soon switchback and start a generally rising traverse of the pasture on the south ridge of Puigmal. Reach a high point (2090m, **1hr 20min**) and veer left, crossing a track. This track provides an easy route up Puigmal.

Turn left along the second track and follow this below a spring providing quality water. The traverse now goes up and down with a high point of 2150m before rejoining the GR11 just before reaching Núria (**1hr 20min**).

GR11 to Núria

The GR11 goes right after crossing the footbridge over Torrent de l'Estremera and soon forks right. Follow the main path, ignoring side turns. The path becomes a bit vague across a grassy area, after which you pass a tiny hut, just about big enough for two people to shelter in a storm. After the hut you descend below big cliffs and pass Font dels Plaus (1510m) just before a farm building. Water. Reach a track and turn left and, soon after a switchback, take a shortcut left which regains the track just before a stream. Turn left and continue along the track, forking right and then right again. Immediately after a switchback, turn sharp left down an old path to a concrete track. Turn left along a path which soon joins the concrete track which leads you into **Queralbs**. Pass the church, Iglesia de Sant Jaume, which has a covered seating area. Water point (1196m, **1hr 20min**).

Queralbs church

Queralbs is a small village with a small shop (which has with a larger selection of food than the Planoles shops) and two hostal bar-restaurants (Hostal L'Avet ca la Mari and Hostal Les Roquetes).

Continue down Carrer de Fond de Dalt and turn left up Camí de Núria. Follow a concrete road until a signpost shows the start of the path to Núria (Camí a Núria). Fork left up a concrete track which soon becomes a path. Turn right at a road, then fork left up a concrete track, forking left up a path just before a gate. Pass a water point. Follow signs to Pont de Cremel at a couple of junctions. You pass the 'Refugi St Pau', a rock overhang under which you could shelter, before reaching the Pont de Cremel. Cross the bridge and continue climbing the right-hand side of the gorge, passing the 'Refugi St Rafael' and 'Refugi St Pere', two more rock overhangs. Cross a stream under a railway bridge and continue up the left-hand side of the valley. Eventually cross a ridge, Creu d'en Riba (1983m). This is where you get your first view of Núria, which looks like a country house that has been transplanted into the mountains. Continue to **Núria** (1967m, **2hr 55min**).

The Sanctuari de Núria is a holiday complex with hotel, youth hostel and basic campground. The shop has minimal food supplies. It is a ski resort in winter and a major tourist attraction in summer. Other attractions include pony trekking, a boating lake, picnic areas, play areas, an excellent interpretive centre, a cafeteria and a selection of bar-restaurants. Access is on foot or by the rack railway from Ribes de Freser or Queralbs.

Núria Alberg (the hostel) is a short walk or cable car journey above Núria.

If you have spare time, you could take an extra day at Núria and use it for a traverse of Puigmal (2910m), the highest mountain in the Pyrenees east of the Cerdanya plateau.

The history of Núria goes back to **Sant Gil**. Sant Gil was a Greek who arrived in the valley in approximately AD700 and lived there for four years. He crafted an image of the Virgin Mary and later hid it in a cave when forced to flee from the Arians, a Christian sect. Legend has it that a pilgrim named Amadéu began searching for the image in 1072, after having a prophetic dream. He built a small chapel for pilgrims and found the carving seven years later, and the place became known as the Sanctuary of the Virgin of Núria. The wooden Romanesque carving, which is still venerated today, has in fact been dated to about 1200.

It was in Núria that the first Catalan Statute of Autonomy was drafted in 1931, and Núria and the surrounding mountains are a popular destination for

Catalans on their National Day, 11 September. This date commemorates the fall of Barcelona to the Bourbon king in 1714, which resulted in the incorporation of Catalonia into Castile in 1716, giving Spain a united administration.

STAGE 39
Núria to Setcases

Start	Núria
Finish	Setcases
Time	6hr
Distance	19.7km
Total ascent	1045m
Total descent	1745m
Difficulty	The walking is easy, but the ridge is not for the inexperienced in bad weather. It would be sensible to make an early start to avoid any possible thunderstorms high up.
High points	Coll de Tirapits (2780m), Col de Noucreus (2785m), Coll de la Marrana (2520m)

Surprisingly, well to the east of the high mountains, the GR11 attains its greatest height as it passes along the border ridge.

From the entrance of the main building, walk NE past the end of the railway. Turn right, cross a bridge, turn left, cross a road and go up a path signed for Noucreus. Climb on the right side of the Torrent de Noucreus and follow a path into the woods above the stream. This path soon climbs up to a track which you follow left, ignoring a right turn to 'Alberg' (the hostel) (**20min**). The track becomes a path by the time you pass the junction of the Torrent de Noufonts and Torrent de Noucreus. Cross the Torrent de Noucreus on a bridge. You could take water here, but a better option is to fill up at 2470m where there are no more cows and the stream emerges from underground. Head N to reach a signed junction (2180m, **20min**).

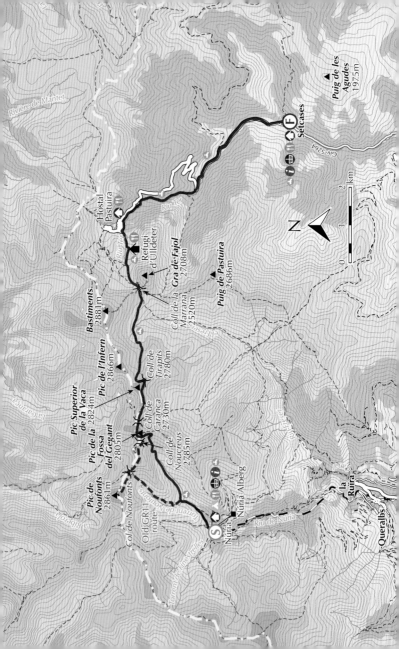

Alternative route

The left turn, signed to Noufonts, is the old route of the GR11, and since it offers great views on the ridge, it is suggested that you follow it in good weather. It adds 30min compared to the present GR11 route. Follow the path up to the **Col de Noufonts** and turn right along the ridge to rejoin the GR11 near the **Coll de Noucreus**. (2785m, **1hr 55min**) There is the added option of climbing the Pic de Noufonts (2861m) to the west of the Coll de Noufonts and the Pic de la Fossa del Gegant between the two cols.

Main route

The GR11 goes right and follows the path above the left-hand bank of the Torrent de Noucreus. Good camping at 2600m. Eventually the path comes close to the stream before veering left and switchbacking up to the **Coll de Noucreus** (2785m, **1hr 25min**) with Borderstone 510, where nine small crosses are embedded in the rock.

> The story goes that the **nine crosses** commemorate nine monks who died here when caught in a storm, but the evidence for this is thin.

The GR11 goes slightly left of the easily climbed **Pic de la Fossa del Gegant** (2805m) with two more crosses. Descend E to **Coll de Caranca** (2730m) and climb to pass S of the summit of **Pic Superior de la Vaca** (2824m) to reach the **Coll de Tirapits** on its SE ridge (2780m, **50min**).

The GR11 swings left (N) from here, forking right below an emergency shelter (not suitable for sleeping in) and then heading down to the left of the probably dry Torrent de les Barranques. Cross a stream. There are plenty of good camping spots between here and the Refugi de Ulldeter. Veer left down to a bigger stream where a variation, the GR11.7, joins from the right (**30min**). The GR11 now makes a rising traverse to the **Coll de la Marrana** (2520m, **25min**).

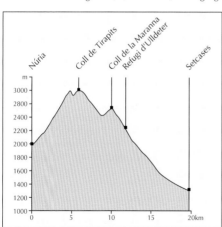

Morning clouds lifting at Coll de Tirapits with the wide Bastiments peak (2881m) behind

Well-trodden paths climb Gra de Fajol (2708m) to the south-east and Bastiments (2881m) to the north-west.

Descend easily down a switchbacking path, then down a well-waymarked broad path, ignoring a left fork, to reach a wide ski piste. Cross this and descend left of it down the ridge to the manned **Refugi d'Ulldeter** (2220m, **25min**). Water point outside.

> Refugi d'Ulldeter, with full refuge facilities, is open from June to mid September and weekends throughout the year.

A well-marked path goes left from the refuge before descending, crossing the stream and heading down a path to car parking on a switchback on the ski road. The GR11 shortcuts the switchbacks as you descend to the left of the stream and then follow the road until just below the bottom car park, then turn sharp right down a footpath (**25min**). **Hostal Pastuira** is just down the road on the left.

> Hostal Pastuira has mountain hut-style accommodation and a bar-restaurant.

The path veers left and joins a rough track which goes down the left-hand side of the Riu Ter stream. Continue down the track until you reach the road at a switchback (**35min**). Follow this road down for 4km, passing a water point on the left (**15min**). After the road crosses the Riu Ter, fork right and walk to the centre of **Setcases** (1265m, **30min**).

> Setcases is a charming village with a large food shop, several bar-restaurants and several hostel bar-restaurants offering accommodation (a selection of these are listed below).

FACILITIES ON STAGE 39

Refugi d'Ulldeter: tel 972 192 004 or 619 514 159 www.ulldeter.es

Setcases Tourist Information: tel 972 136 089

Hostal Pastuira: tel 972 136 043 www.pastuira.com

Hostal-Restaurant Can Tiranda: tel 972 136 052 www.cantiranda.com

Hostal-Restaurant la Cabanya: tel 972 136 065 www.lacabanya.net

Hostal Bar-Restaurant El Moli: tel 972 136 049 www.elmoli.net

Hostal-Restaurant Can Falera: tel 972 136 093
can-falera.catalonia-hotels.com

Hostal-Restaurant Ter: tel 972 136 096 www.hostalter.com

STAGE 40

Setcases to Beget

Start	Setcases
Finish	Beget
Time	6hr 20min
Distance	23.3km
Total ascent	810m
Total descent	1535m
Difficulty	Easy. Waymarking is generally good. The riverside path into Beget can be very slippery when wet.
High point	Summit above Coll de Lliens (1904m)

The GR11 now leaves the high mountains behind and enters a region of steep wooded hills. As you are approaching the Mediterranean Sea you can expect hot dry conditions and you should be particularly careful not to start a wildfire, as the woods are likely to be tinder-dry.

Leave the centre of Setcases on the east side and cross the Pont d'en Jepet, the bridge over the Riu Ter. Turn right past a water point. Veer left on a concrete track which soon turns right over a bridge across the Torrent de Vall-Llobre. Follow a

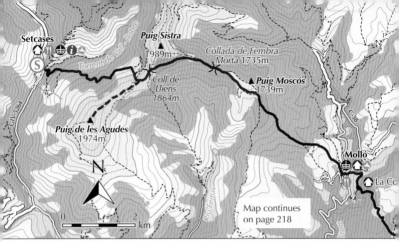

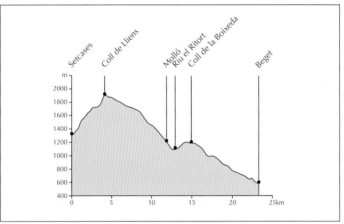

steep track which switchbacks up the hill. Ignore a path off on the right and a track which goes straight on at a switchback. Continue climbing until a path goes off left (**25min**). Turn left along this path and pass through grassy areas (**20min**). This is the first feasible dry camping on the ascent. You cross several small streams. The water should be treated before drinking as there are cows in this area. Turn left (**25min**) and cross a large grassy area before joining a grassy track. When you reach a large grassy area (**15min**) turn right straight up the hillside to reach a path (**10min**). Turn left and immediately right at the switchback of a grassy track and continue climbing. When you reach a grassy area just below the ridge, veer left along a line of poles. Excellent dry campsites. Puig de les Agudes (1975m) to the south-west is an easy walk from here.

When you reach the fence, follow it left over a grassy top (1904m, **15min**) and down to the **Coll de Lliens** (1864m) with a signpost. Cross the fence and go diagonally right along a path which contours the south face of Puig Sistra (1985m). Fork right (**15min**) and ignore a path leading to the GR10 in France. On returning to the fence on the ridge, follow it down to the **Collada de Fembra Morta** (1735m), where the path contours the southern slopes of Puig Moscós. You could follow the fence over the summit of Puig Moscós (1740m) and regain the GR11 by its south-east ridge.

When you next meet the fence, cross it and keep straight on to reach a fence on the next ridge. Cross the fence and turn right along it, soon veering left down a track. Good dry campsites. Fork right, then turn right after crossing another fence and continue roughly S down the ridge. Fork left to arrive at a junction just before a house (**1hr**). Go straight on and pass La Font del Rossinyol at the house. Water point. Continue downhill SE, pass a tiny picnic area at Font d'en Tornet (water point) and walk into **Molló** (1184m, **20min**). Water point.

Tiny Maria chapel above Molló

Molló has two food shops, several bar-restaurants and a hotel (Hotel Calitxó).

In the village, ignore the first street on your left and go left at the second street, Carrer dels Castanyers. Go down with the church on your left, cross a road and go down to the C-38 road. Cross this road too and go diagonally left down a track, soon turning right down an old path, passing between two houses and continuing downhill to an old bridge across the El Ritort (1050m, **15min**) with a swimming hole. Don't cross the bridge, but turn right and follow a concrete track downstream, past another bridge and then down to another bridge (**5min**) with more swimming holes. Cross the bridge and continue on the track and climb, ignoring side turns.

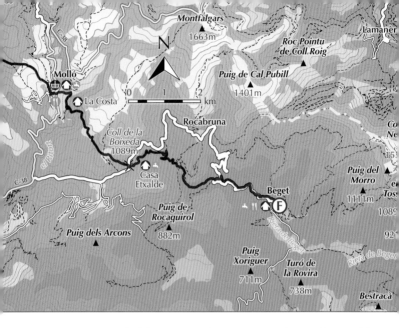

Pass **La Costa**, which has accommodation. Keep straight on at the top of the hill and follow the track, which is grassy in places, to a junction at Collet de la Costa (**35min**) at the top of another hill. Go straight on through a gate and across a field to another gate. Go down immediately to cross a (dry) streambed, then go E across the next field to pick up a path which reaches a track at a switchback. Fork right to the **Coll de la Boixeda** (1089m, **10min**).

Cross the road and take the path E at a seating area, descending to Can Serra. Water point. You quickly reach **Casa Etxalde** with accommodation (**10min**). Follow the dirt road until a switchback where the GR11 goes straight on down a grass track (**10min**). Follow the track as it veers left, turning right along a major track which switchbacks down past Can Planas (830m, **15min**). Soon after, when the dirt road goes sharp left, turn right down a path and veer left to farm buildings.

Continue down between the buildings, descend along a stream and eventually cross it. Follow the path on the other side to a road (**35min**). Turn left and after 100m turn right down a path (signpost). This takes you down to the Riera de Beget, which you cross on a wooden bridge over a gorge. Follow the path downstream above the gorge and return to the road (**20min**). Go straight across, follow a path and turn right on returning to the road. After 100m turn left down a path and follow it to **Beget**. Follow Carrer Bell Aire to the village centre (540m, **20min**). There is a seating area by the church. Two water points.

Beget is a hamlet with a choice of accommodation and a bar-restaurant.

FACILITIES ON STAGE 40

Hotel restaurant Calitxó: tel 972 740 386 www.hotelcalitxo.com

Casa Rural La Costa: tel 670 658 983 www.lacostademollo.com

Casa Etxalde: tel 972 130 317 www.etxalde.net

Hostal el Forn: tel 972 741 230 www.elforndebeget.com

STAGE 41
Beget to Sant Aniol d'Aguja

Start	Beget
Finish	Sant Aniol d'Aguja
Time	4hr 25min
Distance	15.7km
Total ascent	750m
Total descent	840m
Difficulty	Easy walking, but limestone paths could be slippery when wet.
High points	Coll dels Muls (700m), Talaixà (760m)

We are now at lower altitude and you must be prepared for high temperatures. A new refuge has been under construction at Sant Aniol d'Aguja for many years and it may still take several years to complete. Until it is complete, Stages 41 and 42 will need to be combined into a very long day; alternatively you will have to stay at the new refuge at Talaixà, which has accommodation but no meals service.

Follow the signs for GR11, veering right from the church and down a track. Turn left when you reach the main road and follow it across a bridge. Continue along the road to the next bridge (**15min**). Don't cross but turn left up a concrete farm track, soon forking right and following the main track, ignoring side turns. Good, dry campsites 30min from Beget. Fork right at a signed junction (**40min**), cross the

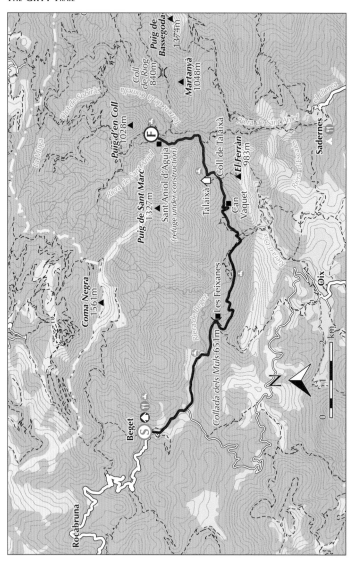

river and bear left. When the track veers left, at La Farga, go straight on along a small path, cross a (dry) streambed and start climbing. Cross the **Coll dels Muls**

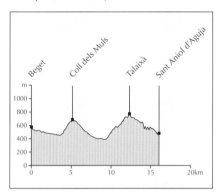

(651m) and pass through an old courtyard at Les Feixanes, a ruined farm (680m, **30min**). Fork left and follow the main track, ignoring side turns. Start switchbacking down to reach a large open area. Good, dry camping. Fork right at the bottom of the open area and continue descending, ignoring several tracks off to the left, to reach the Riera de Beget at some gates (**35min**). Follow the track to the right of the river. Pass through a grassy area with a (private) covered picnic area to the right. Pass a little spring on your right which, if running, will provide better quality water than that in the river. Continue to a signpost by another grassy area, the Pla de la Plantada (370m, **15min**), just before some gates. Camping is possible at either grassy area.

Sant Martí de Talaixà

Turn left, cross a bridge over the stream and follow the path which climbs to a track. Turn right and after a couple of minutes turn right again up a path which at first is more like a gully. Turn right at a track (**40min**) and follow switchbacks uphill to a ruined farmhouse, **Can Vaquet** (**15min**). Turn left up a path immediately before the farmhouse. Ignore lots of side turns off this well-marked path and cross a track and climb to **Coll de Talaixà** (760m, **25min**).

> In the large building here there is a free part on the left (Cal Ferrer) as well as a bookable part (minimum two nights) on the right. Water point (rainwater reservoir) and camping.

Be careful to follow the correct waymarked path as you leave the pass and roughly contour on this old path until you reach the ruins of La Quera (**15min**). The waymarks lead you between the buildings, then fork left up a track and fork left again to regain the path. Follow the ancient path on a slowly descending traverse of the steep south-east ridge of Puig de Sant Marc (1327m), often seeming to cling to the rock face; the traverse has a few ups as well as downs. There is a final descent to **Sant Aniol d'Aguja** (450m, **35min**). Water point. No camping.

> **Sant Aniol d'Aguja** is the remains of a Benedictine monastery which was established in the 9th century and is very popular with tourists. The stream just below is good for cooling off in hot weather. Sant Aniol d'Aguja is being restored but the works on a new refuge seem to be a long-term project. At the time of writing completion dates are unknown.

FACILITIES ON STAGE 41

Talaixà: www.ceolot.cat/casa-de-talaixa

STAGE 42
Sant Aniol d'Aguja to Albanyà

Start	Sant Aniol d'Aguja
Finish	Albanyà
Time	5hr 10min
Distance	18.2km
Total ascent	785m
Total descent	995m
Difficulty	Easy
High points	Coll Roig (840m), Coll de Principi (1126m)

The two best swimming holes on the GR11 are on this stage. Both are about five minutes off the trail.

Take the path left of the church down to the Riera de Sant Aniol, cross the bridge and follow the path on the other side. There are lots of side turns so watch the waymarks carefully. After 5min there are grassy clearings on your right where camping is possible. Continue to a signed path junction. If you turn right, you will come to a swimming hole in about 5min which is better than any others on the GR11. If you have some spare time, it is worth considering a trip down to Sadernes.

Sadernes has a campground with a small shop and a bar-restaurant. There is also a guesthouse, El Vilarot.

The Riera de Sant Aniol flows down a **dramatic limestone gorge**, which is the main reason so many tourists walk up to Sant Aniol from Sadernes (70min down, 85min up without pack).

Hikers at the Sant Aniol d'Aguja monastery

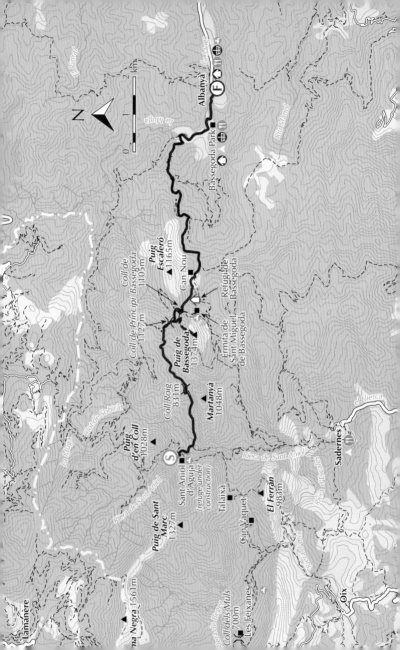

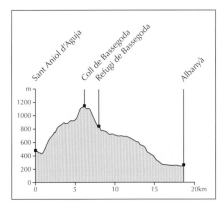

Turn left, signed to Albanyà (**10min**), and then turn right across the Torrent de la Comella, after which the path climbs steadily to a viewpoint (**40min**). After a short respite you continue climbing to **Coll Roig** (831m, **30min**). Here, you will find the first dry camping opportunity since the meadows after Sant Aniol d'Aguja. The path contours briefly ENE from Coll Roig before starting a gradually rising traverse. Soon fork right down a path. Cross a (dry) streambed and turn right along a track before forking left off it. Climb to a grassy area with some ruins. The path may not be clear, but it stays left of both the grassy area and the ruins and climbs steeply to a dirt road (**20min**). Turn right and soon reach **Coll de Principi** (1127m). Start descending on a dirt road and almost immediately fork left. The right fork is for the ascent of Puig de Bassegoda. Continue to the **Coll de Bassegoda** (1105m, **1hr 5min**). Good, dry camping.

Ascent of Puig de Bassegoda

Puig de Bassegoda (1374m) to the south-west is your last chance to climb a 'mountain' on the GR11. Either follow the track from the Coll de Principi or

Puig d'en Coll from Coll Roig

a (yellow) waymarked path from the Coll de Bassegoda, which soon joins the track. Continue to the track end (**10min**). Excellent dry campsites. Head straight up the hill on a path marked by cairns and green waymarks. Ignore paths going to the right. The final climb is an easy scramble up a limestone buttress with the aid of iron rungs (35min up, 25min down). There are magnificent views to the remainder of the GR11 and the Mediterranean to the north-west in France, as well as back to the high mountains.

Main route continues
Fork right at the pass and turn sharp left after 150m. Follow a well-marked rocky path which switchbacks steeply down through the wood to the **Refugi de Bassegoda** (820m, **30min**). The **Ermita de Sant Miguel de Bassegoda** is 200m west of the hut, where there is a water point.

> This large unmanned refuge (20 places) is well maintained but is kept locked to avoid vandalism. It can be booked for a small fee via refugis@cee.cat or by calling 620 90 15 60. You will then get a number code to unlock the door.

The GR11 now roughly contours to **Can Nou** and goes round the right-hand side of the farmhouse to its entrance at the bottom. Follow the dirt road E from Can Nou past a usually dry fountain. When you reach a concrete road (**10min**), turn left and follow it all the way to Albanyà. There are some shortcuts, with yellow waymarks, which you could take across some of the switchbacks if you like steep slippery paths. Eventually reach a junction at the bottom of the hill (**1hr 20min**). It is worth turning left here to find a magnificent swimming hole in La Muga a few minutes upstream, where a concrete ramp leads down to the river. Turn right for the GR11 and follow the road downstream to **Bassegoda Park campground** (**15min**).

> Bassegoda Park campground, which has cabins too, is about 1km west of Albanyà. It has a bar-restaurant and a small supermarket which stocks 'original' and 'easy-clic' camping gas.

Continue down the road to a GR11 noticeboard in **Albanyà** (237m, **10min**). All facilities are to your right.

> Albanyà is a small village with a bar-restaurant and a small shop with limited supplies. La Rectoria d'Albanyà offers accommodation, bar and meals. There are a couple of casas rurales about 1km east of the village. The Font de l'Olla is also behind the church.

FACILITIES ON STAGE 42

Càmping Masia Sadernes: tel 972 687 536 www.sadernes.com

El Vilarot: 649 866 085 www.elvilarot.com

Bassegoda Park campground: tel 972 542 020
www.bassegodapark.com

Refugi de Bassegoda: tel 620 901 560 www.cee.cat/bassegoda/

Can Carreras: tel 620 335 862 www.cancarreras.com

Can Mas Albanyà: tel 972 542 023 www.canmasalbanya.com

La Rectoria d'Albanyà: tel 872 202 644 www.rectoriadalbanya.com

---

STAGE 43
Albanyà to Maçanet de Cabrenys

Start	Albanyà
Finish	Maçanet de Cabrenys
Time	4hr 45min
Distance	19.7km
Total ascent	780m
Total descent	670m
Difficulty	Easy
High point	East ridge, Puig de la Trilla (690m)

The GR11 continues through steep wooded hills.

After visiting Albanyà, return to the GR11 noticeboard. Continue E down a narrow concrete road, the Camí de Maçanet, with water point. Immediately after the last house, turn left up a track. When the track veers right, fork left up a path (**10min**) and climb steeply to a track junction (**20min**). Take the track that goes diagonally right uphill and, after a couple of minutes, fork right up a path, shortcutting the track. On rejoining the track, turn right and immediately left for the next shortcut. Then it's left along the track, forking right to reach a junction as you reach the ridge at a crossroad (566m, **25min**). Turn right and follow the track to pass an

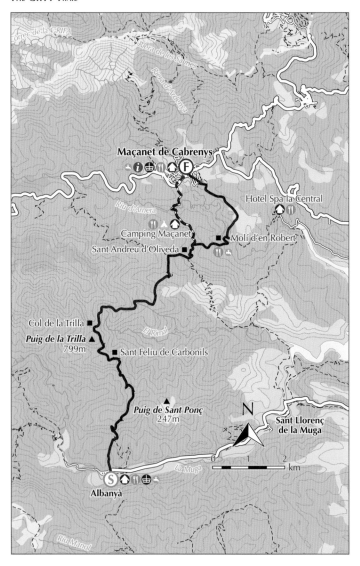

Maçanet de Cabrenys

Hotel Spa la Central

Camping Maçanet

Molí d'en Robert

Sant Andreu d'Oliveda

Col de la Trilla

Puig de la Trilla
799m

Sant Feliu de Carbonils

El Rimal

Puig de Sant Ponç
247m

Sant Llorenç
de la Muga

N

0   1   2 km

Albanyà

Riu d'Arnera

Rera de les Salines

Torrec. de la GRILA

La Muga

Riu Manol

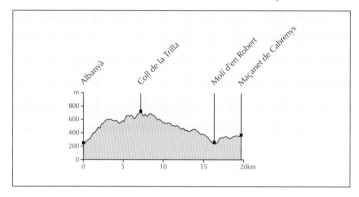

ornate gate (**15min**). Fork left soon after this and left again. Pass the **Església de Sant Feliu de Carbonils** (**40min**) on your right. Dry camping.

The GR11 keeps straight on and follows the main track. Soon pass through a metal gate with a sign which indicates that you are entering private land, but GR hikers are allowed through. Ignore several side turns as the road passes right of Puig de la Trilla to reach a grassy area. Dry camping possible. Go straight on at Coll de la Trilla (692m, **30min**) where the road turns sharply left. Go onto a path which goes right past the buildings at **La Trilla** and, at a switchback, keep straight on (ENE) for an undulating traverse. Soon cross a forest track, cross the probably dry El Rimal and eventually reach a small hilltop (**40min**). Camping possible.

Pass a ruined farm, where the path becomes a track, and drop down to a larger track. Turn left, then shortly afterwards fork right and then turn left SSW along a path. This path soon veers steeply downhill to a small woodland stream. Cross the stream further down and follow the path as it descends above the left-hand bank and then starts to climb away from it. Soon fork left up a faint, easily missed path (**25min**) and climb steeply to a dirt road. Turn right and reach a junction, signed to Sant Andreu d'Oliveda (**15min**). Turn right and soon go straight across a six-way junction. Turn left along the main dirt road and left again to join a tarmac road at **Sant Andreu d'Oliveda** (**15min**). Follow the road and soon reach a junction.

Camping Maçanet de Cabrenys (cabins, a bar-restaurant and camping) is about 1km along the tarmac road. You can then follow the road a further 3km to Maçanet de Cabrenys.

A refreshing swim is an option near Molí d'en Robert

Fork right down the dirt road for the GR11, ignoring the sign to Maçanet de Cabrenys. Cross a stream with rock pools (good for swimming) as you reach the **Restaurant Molí d'en Robert**, which has a swimming pool (**20min**). Water, but no camping.

Turn left onto a path, then right along a track after the final building, and then turn immediately left onto a path which leads through a cork oak forest on the way to a plateau. Keep straight on along the middle track at a track junction (**10min**) then turn left at a junction and follow the dirt road, ignoring lots of side turns. This becomes a tarmac road at the edge of **Maçanet de Cabrenys**. A way-marked route takes you through the outskirts and across a bridge to a junction with the main road (GI-503) (**20min**).

Maçanet de Cabrenys is a large village with a tourist information office, three hotels, casas rurales, bar-restaurants and several small shops. You pass a water point, Font del Carrer Llarg, as you head into the village.

FACILITIES ON STAGE 43

Restaurant El Molí d'en Robert: tel 972 544 004
www.elmolidenrobert.com

Camping Maçanet de Cabrenys: tel 667 776 648
www.campingmassanet.com

Hotel Spa la Central: tel 972 535 053 www.hotelspalacentral.com

Maçanet de Cabrenys Tourist Information Office: tel 972 544 297

Hostal La Quadra: tel 972 544 032 www.laquadra.com

Hotel Els Caçadors De Maçanet: tel 972 544 136
www.hotelelscassadors.com

Can Mach: tel 972 543 311 www.canmach.com

STAGE 44

Maçanet de Cabrenys to La Jonquera

Start	Maçanet de Cabrenys
Finish	La Jonquera
Time	5hr 10min
Distance	23.1km
Total ascent	555m
Total descent	790m
Difficulty	Easy. Well waymarked.
High point	Puig de la Creu (600m)

Campsites are few and far between in this rocky terrain. Camping at Eugènia may well be your best option.

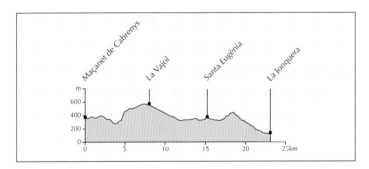

The GR11 goes ENE along the GI-503 road to a picnic area and GR11 information board at the edge of the village. Fork left up a track and, when the main track goes left, keep straight on along a rough track. Descend through a bouldery cork oak forest, go down to a dry riverbed, cross it and climb up on the other side. Ignore several side paths and reach a track (**20min**). Turn left, follow this track for 150m and turn right onto a wide path which gradually turns narrower. Follow this path until an unclear junction with an improvised sign (330m, **20min**). The main path continues north to El Suro de la Pubilla (a monumental oak tree), but you turn sharply right. Soon reach La Font del Bruc. Water point. Turn right at the next junction to arrive back at the GI-503 (260m, **10min**).

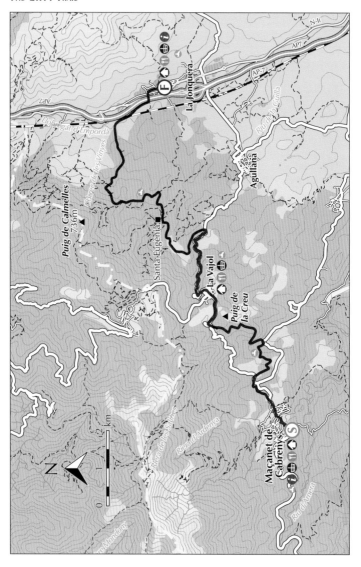

Turn left across the bridge and shortly afterwards turn left onto a path. Fork right and climb steeply. As you near the top of the hill you reach a small track (**30min**). Turn right, then left and then fork right, skirting W of the summit of **Puig de la Creu**. This track takes you to a large building above the Canta Mine (**25min**) where you fork right to a road (521m, **5min**). Turn right and follow the road to a picnic site just above La Vajol. Water point.

La Vajol is a small village with two bar-restaurants which also offer accommodation. Ca la Conxita also has a tiny shop.

Continue down the road through the hamlet, passing Ca la Conxita bar-restaurant (**10min**) and a water point near a monument. Reach the car park at the bottom of **La Vajol** and follow the main road (GI-501) down for about 3.5km, until a dirt road goes off sharp left signed to Santa Eugènia (**40min**). Turn left along this dirt road. There's an area just before Capella de Can Brell where you could camp. Fork right just before a house and continue along the road to **Santa Eugènia** (350m, **45min**), a large chapel with a side building that is sometimes in use as a youth camp hostel. Water point at the showers next to the swimming pool.

Take the track heading E and follow the waymarked main track at junctions. Pass right of a field then descend gently before climbing steadily to a high point (430m, **40min**). Turn right and immediately left, ignoring several side turns, before

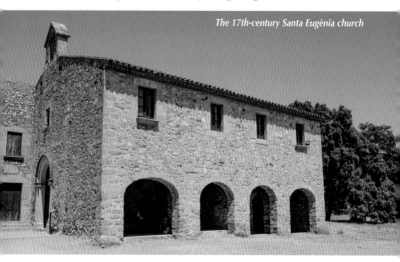

The 17th-century Santa Eugènia church

turning right at a junction with signpost (**15min**). Turn right alongside a fence at a junction at the bottom of the hill (**20min**), veering left and following the track under the railway. Turn right and eventually left through a tunnel under the motorway to arrive at **La Jonquera** (114m, **25min**). Go straight on, cross the river and turn right down the main street, Carrer Major, until a small square, Plaça de l'Ajuntament, is reached (**5min**).

La Jonquera is a busy border town with a lot of large supermarkets to serve cross-border traffic, as well as many smaller shops, hotels and bar-restaurants. In both Sol Jonquera Supermercado and Stop Centre Commercial, 'original' and 'easy-clic' camping gas are found.

FACILITIES ON STAGE 44

Ca la Conxita: tel 972 535 213 www.calaconxita.com

Casa Comaulis: tel 972 535 175

La Jonquera Tourist Office: tel 972 514 431

Hotel Tramuntana: tel 972 556 558 www.hoteltramuntana.com

Hotel Frontera: tel 972 554 050 www.hotelfrontera.es

Font del Pla Hotel Restaurant: tel 972 556 393 www.fontdelpla.net

STAGE 45
La Jonquera to Els Vilars

Start	La Jonquera
Finish	Els Vilars
Time	6hr 35min
Distance	25.1km
Total ascent	995m
Total descent	890m
Difficulty	Easy and well waymarked. The heat could be the biggest problem. An early start is recommended.
High points	Puig dels Falguers (778m), Coll de la Llosarda (690m)

The only staffed accommodation on this stage is in Requesens. At Els Vilars there are no facilities apart from a water point. This is where walkers requiring accommodation will need to divert from the GR11, on the alternative route described in Stage 46, to find accommodation in Espolla or Rabós. For campers there are several options and there is also a well-maintained hut just after Requesens.

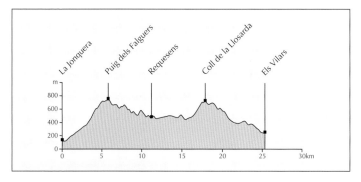

Climb to Ermita de Santa Llúcia

From the Plaça de l'Ajuntament turn left up an alleyway, Carrer Sant Miquel, then first right and first left up Carrer Migdia. Veer right up Carrer Rosselló and fork left up Camí de Santa Llúcia. Fork left again and, at the end of the fenced properties, turn left up a path (**10min**). The GR11 now follows a complicated but well-waymarked combination of paths and tracks to arrive at a picnic table and good water point, Font de la Soula (**50min**).

Climb steps to **Ermita de Santa Llúcia** (435m), with a covered shelter, suitable for a bivouac. The chapel, the main picnic site, another shelter and a fine viewpoint are on your right. The GR11 follows waymarks up a path to the left. This sometimes rough or eroded path climbs steadily, eventually

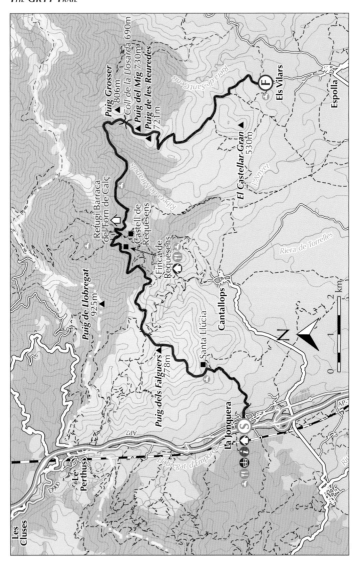

Puig Grosser
806m

Coll de la Llosarda 690m

Puig del Mig 730m

Puig de les Reuredes
721m

Ribera de Sant Genís

Els Vilars

Espolla

El Castellar-Gran
530m

Torrelles

Ribera de Maçanell

Refugi Barraca
del Forn de Calç

Castell de
Requesens

Finca de
Requesens

Riera de Torrelles

Puig de Llobregat
925m

Cantallops

Santa Llúcia

N

km

Puig dels Falguers
778m

Santa Llúcia

La Jonquera

S

AP7

Les
Perthus

Llobregat d'Empordà

AP

Les
Cluses

236

reaching a col (**1hr 5min**). Continue up the ridge to cross the summit plateau of **Puig dels Falguers** (778m, **10min**).

Continue roughly NE along a small path, cross a grassy col and continue over rocky terrain to a track junction (**15min**). Turn right along a major track. Seven to eight minutes later you should see above you the almost complete remains of a DC-6, which crashed into the trees in 1986. A short distance further on a plaque on the right commemorates the French aircrew who lost their lives in the crash. Continue along the track, passing a water point on the left on your approach to the sanctuary and **hostel-restaurant at Requesens** (500m, **50min**).

Finca de Requesens is a small hostel-restaurant in a unique setting in the Catalan hills.

Follow the track N, soon passing a fountain with a picnic table. Water point. At the next switchback go straight on, signed to Els Vilars (**10min**). Cross a trickling stream and fork right, then bear left at a junction before switchbacking right as you cross another woodland stream. Soon fork left and then turn left when you meet a wall. Soon pass the **Refugi Barraca del Forn de Calç**, a small unstaffed hut (six places, **15min**), left of the path. Possible water from rainwater tank. Veer right then fork left and follow this track, which twists and turns. Cross another trickling woodland stream and eventually pass to the left of the ruins of Mas Mirapols (**35min**).

In a few minutes cross a woodland stream, then climb steadily and cross another woodland stream (**20min**). Take the path that veers right from here. When a ridge is reached the path veers left and climbs a little way up the ridge before contouring right, signed to Vilamaniscle. You soon reach the open south-western ridge of **Puig Grosser** (806m) at **Coll de la Llosarda** (690m, **25min**).

Contour right of **Puig del Mig** (730m), cross the fence at the next saddle and contour left of **Puig de les Reuredes** (721m) before descending through the woods to a track (**20min**). Turn right and switchback down, ignoring any side turns. Keep straight on at a junction with good campsites (**25min**) and pass the almost certainly dry Font de la Verna. Ignore a sign, 'Els Vilars 0.7km', and stay on the main track to a junction as you approach **Els Vilars**, then turn right to reach the hamlet (220m, **45min**). The water point is at the roadhead at the bottom of the hamlet.

FACILITIES ON STAGE 45

Finca de Requesens: tel 646 179 509 www.fincaderequesens.cat

STAGE 46

Els Vilars to Llançà (GR11)

Start	Els Vilars
Finish	Llançà
Time	5hr 30min
Distance	26.1km
Total ascent	565m
Total descent	790m
Difficulty	Easy. The heat could be the biggest problem and could make this into a longer hike than anticipated. An early start is recommended.
High points	Coll de la Plaja (395m), Coll de la Serra (260m), Coll de les Portes (230m)

The approach to the Mediterranean is through hot, dry hills. The GR11 follows a route with an excess of road walking north on the way to Vilamaniscle. The alternative Stage 46A also involves a little less road walking and offers a shorter way to Vilamaniscle.

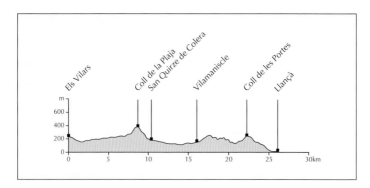

As the track turns right on the northern edge of the Els Vilars, follow an indistinct path left. The path goes right of a dry stream, crosses it and then veers right along a wall before crossing the stream again.

A clear path descends the left-hand side of the (dry) stream, forking left to reach Font de Cadecàs, with a picnic table but probably no water (**15min**). Fork left up the track and soon cross a stream. Reach a tarmac road (**10min**), turn left and follow it for the next 5km, steadily climbing to pass Mas Girarols and the dolmens of Girarols before reaching the ruins of **Mas Pils** at a junction of roads (250m, **1hr**).

Turn right down a track and cross a (dry) stream. Good, dry campsites. Continue until a path goes off right when the track bends left (**20min**). Climb the possibly overgrown path to Fonteta II and up to Fonteta I. Water points. Turn right when you regain the track to arrive at the **Coll de la Plaja** (390m, **15min**). Keep straight on until a footpath shortcuts left (**15min**), going straight across the track when you meet it again, then turning right along it to reach the Convento de Sant Quirze de Colera (165m, **10min**). The church dates back to at least the 9th century.

There is a bar-restaurant just up the track on the left, open until 5pm, but closed Tuesdays and Wednesdays. There is a water point behind the convent.

Follow the dirt road, soon to become a tarmac road, to a road junction (**50min**). Stage 46a via Espolla rejoins from the right. The GR11 goes left, passing through vineyards to reach a water point, Font de l'Ou, with seating area and GR11 information board, as you arrive in **Vilamaniscle** (155m, **20min**).

Vilamaniscle has very limited facilities for walkers. There is a casa rural, a small shop and the swimming pool has a bar. There is a bivouac area below the swimming pool.

Turn left at the water point and climb steeply before turning right along Carrer Tramuntana, passing the Font del Suro (probably the last water point before Llançà), and then pass the Cases de Colonies Tramuntana – a youth camp – at the top of the village (**5min**). The road now becomes a dirt road which is followed to the Coll de la Serra (260m, **20min**). Turn left, then, at the second switchback, keep straight on down a smaller track and contour along this track. As the track eventually starts descending, a path goes off left (**25min**) and drops steeply down to the Església de Sant Silvestre de Valleta (**5min**). The chapel dates back to the 10th century.

Follow the dirt road down from the chapel. After a couple of minutes pass the Font del Xac, just across the (dry) streambed on your right. Continue to a junction with a concrete track then turn sharp left. This track gradually veers right as it climbs through abandoned terraces to reach the **Coll de les Portes** (230m, **25min**). Keep straight on to the next col (**5min**) where the descent to **Llançà** begins. Follow the track to pass under the railway (**30min**) on the outskirts of town. Turn left after the bridge along a very broad dirt road to arrive at the main road. Cross the road to Llançà Tourist Office (**5min**). There is a water point in the park behind the tourist office.

The campground is located in the north part of the town, near the railway. There is a supermarket and bar (no restaurant).

FACILITIES ON STAGE 46

Restaurant El Corral de Sant Quirze: tel 972 193 186

Can Salas: tel 660 154 747 www.cansalasespolla.com

Casa Rural Cal Sisco: tel 647 842 765

Alberg Costa Brava: tel 616 433 588 www.albergcostabrava.com

Pensió-restaurant Llançà: tel 972 380 160 www.pensionllanca.com

Camping l'Ombra: tel 972 380 335 www.campinglombra.com

Llançà Tourist Information Office: tel 972 380 855 www.visitllanca.cat

Ripe figs are usually easy to find close to the Mediterranean Sea

STAGE 46A
Els Vilars to Llançà (via Espolla and Rabós)

Start	Els Vilars
Finish	Llançà
Time	4hr 35min (2hr 35min to Vilamaniscle)
Distance	20.5km (10.5km to Vilamaniscle)
Total ascent	420m
Total descent	630m
Difficulty	Easy, but there is no waymarking as it is not a recognised route. The heat could be the biggest problem. An early start is recommended.
High point	Col de la Serra (260m)
Note	This route is about 1hr faster compared to Stage 46. For map see Stage 46.

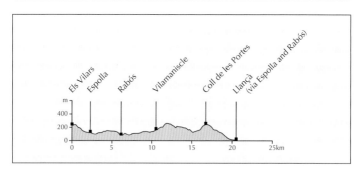

Leave the GR11 and follow the track through Els Vilars to the water point at the bottom of the hamlet. Join a tarmac road and follow it S to **Espolla**. Fork left of the church and then turn right, round the edge of the village, until just before a rough parking area (130m, **30min**). Turn right for Can Salas and other facilities in Espolla.

> Espolla has a turisme rural, Can Salas, plus several hotels, small shops and bar-restaurants.

Vineyard on the edge of Espolla

Otherwise turn left (E) along a concrete track, signed to Rabós and Vilamaniscle. Ignore lots of minor tracks and eventually the track becomes a dirt track. Continue along the main track, pass a concrete driveway to a house on a ridge and reach a four-way junction under electricity wires at **Col Fornell**. Turn right and follow the track, which becomes a concrete track just before you fork right down a tarmac road to arrive at **Rabós** (116m, **55min**).

> Rabós has a small supermarket and a casa rural, Cal Gerani. Mas Tres Puig, an organic farm which has a campsite, is located just outside Rabós on the other side of the bridge across l'Orlina del Puig as you leave the village.

Fork left at the square and drop down to a bridge at the eastern edge of the hamlet (6km). There is a water point just before the bridge. Cross the bridge and go diagonally right across the road onto a concrete path that climbs up. A signpost to Vilamaniscle shows the way. Walk in between vineyards on a path and soon notice the upper end of the Mas Tres Puig campsite on your right (**10min**). The track goes down as it turns left (**5min**) and then sharp right. Cross a small stream, La Reguerada, and climb up again. Reach a track, turn left, soon reach another track and turn left again. Go through a gate and continue straight on through a vineyard. Turn left when you have a private property sign on your right side. Go through the next gate to reach an asphalt road where you rejoin the GR11 (**40min**). Turn left and walk to **Vilamaniscle** (**15min**).

Llançà

Turn left at the water point and climb steeply before turning right along Carrer Tramuntana, passing the Font del Suro (probably the last water point before Llançà), and then pass the Cases de Colonies Tramuntana – a youth camp – at the top of the village (**5min**). The road now becomes a dirt road which is followed to the Coll de la Serra (260m, **20min**). Turn left, then – at the second switchback – keep straight on down a smaller track and contour along this track. As the track eventually starts descending, a path goes off left (**25min**) and drops steeply down to the Església de Sant Silvestre de Valleta (**5min**). The chapel dates back to the 10th century.

Follow the dirt road down from the chapel. After a couple of minutes pass the Font del Xac, just across the (dry) streambed on your right. Continue to a junction with a concrete track then turn sharp left. This track gradually veers right as it climbs through abandoned terraces to reach the **Coll de les Portes** (**25min**). Keep straight on to the next col (**5min**) where the descent to **Llançà** begins. Follow the track to pass under the railway (**30min**) on the outskirts of town. Turn left after the bridge along a very broad dirt road to arrive at the main road. Cross the road to Llançà Tourist Office (**5min**). There is a water point in the park behind the tourist office.

FACILITIES ON STAGE 46

Can Salas: tel 660 154 747 www.cansalasespolla.com

Casa Rural Cal Sisco: tel 647 842 765

Mas Tres Puig: tel 696 673 009 www.mastrespuig.com

Casa Rural Cal Sisco: tel 647 842 765

Alberg Costa Brava: tel 616 433 588 www.albergcostabrava.com

Pensió-restaurant Llançà: tel 972 380 160 www.pensionllanca.com

Camping l'Ombra: tel 972 380 335 www.campinglombra.com

Llançà Tourist Information Office: tel 972 380 855 www.visitllanca.cat

STAGE 47

Llançà to Cap de Creus

Start	Llançà
Finish	Cap de Creus
Time	7hr 35min
Distance	27.7km
Total ascent	1015m
Total descent	1015m
Difficulty	Easy. Again the heat could slow you down considerably.
High point	Sant Pere de Rodes (520m)
Note	Few hikers will stay at Cap de Creus, so it's a good idea to plan how you will move on from there. There is a regular bus service to Cadaqués, where there is a choice of accommodation and a bus station with connections to other destinations.

This stage starts with a 500m climb to Sant Pere de Rodes before descending to El Port de la Selva, followed by a path through dry scrub to the peninsula of Cap de Creus on the Mediterranean Sea.

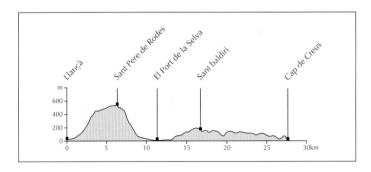

Go left of the tourist office and turn left at the roundabout onto Carrer de la Crue. Take the second street on your right, Carrer de l'Era and follow this street all the way to a T-junction. Turn right and soon turn right again and go onto a path leading to a roundabout. Go right across and follow the right of two small tracks,

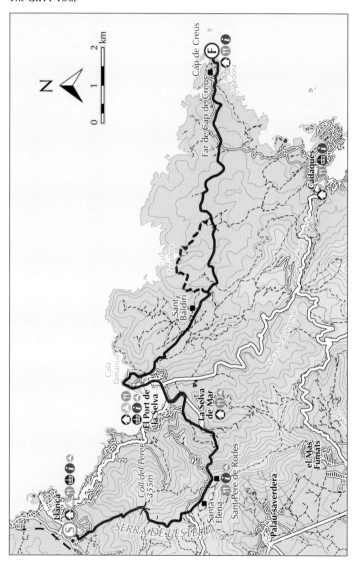

signed for Coll de Perer. The track soon becomes a path, going in between stone walls and leading to a path junction on the Coll del Perer (361m, **1hr 10min**). Turn right and climb to the Serra de l'Estella ridge (462m, **20min**). Turn left along a track, forking left to reach a road junction. Keep straight on along the middle road, signed to St Pere de Rodes, passing the **Església de Santa Elena** to arrive at the popular tourist attraction of the **Monasterio de Sant Pere de Rodes** with café-restaurant (520m, **35min**).

The first authenticated mention of the **monastery** site dates from 878 when there was a simple monastic cell dedicated to St Peter. By 945 this had developed into a Benedictine monastery, which reached its peak in the 11th and 12th centuries when it became an important point of pilgrimage. The monastery declined in the 17th century before being abandoned in 1793. It was declared a National Monument in 1930 with restoration starting in 1935.

Follow the concrete track forking down left, immediately left of the monastery. Follow the concrete track to a car park (**5min**). Descend steeply on the right side of the car park to reach a track (**30min**). Follow the path straight across this track and descend left of a dry gully to reach the Església de Sant Sebastià. Pass right of the cemetery next to the church to enter **La Selva de Mar**.

La Selva de Mar is a hamlet with several bars and restaurants. Bar-restaurant Fonda Felip also offers accommodation.

Turn along the left-hand side of the (possibly dry) stream and pass a water point, Font Mollor. Turn right across an arched bridge and immediately left. Then turn left down an alley and right along the stream. Go left down stone stairs to cross the stream and follow a small path along the left-hand bank. Fork left along a track then left up a path along olive gardens which climbs to another track. Turn right and follow this track to the road descending from Sant Pere. Stay right of the barrier and descend right on a path, then left along a track to reach the GI-6121 road. Turn left along the path beside the road to reach **El Port de la Selva** by Hostal l'Arola, where there is also a campsite (**45min**). Turn right and follow the GR11 along the seafront to reach the main beach. Water points and beach showers.

El Port de la Selva has all the facilities you would expect of a seaside tourist resort, including three campgrounds (listed below) and a wide choice of accommodation. It will be very busy in high season.

Follow the road along the seafront and above the small beaches to the north of the town. Water point. When the coast road starts descending to Cala Tamariua – with its small, sandy beach, where bathing costumes are optional – fork right up a road and climb up. Turn left at the next junction and follow a track going off left at the next junction, where signs indicate you are entering Parc Natural de Cap de Creus. (**40min**). Ignore a right turn to Costa de Oratori and further on turn right at a junction and soon take the second track on the left. Keep straight on when the main track switchbacks and keep straight on again at a complex junction to arrive at the remains of the **Hermitage of Sant Baldiri de Taballera** (**35min**).

The track now veers right as a path and – after a few twists and turns – follows a wall, before forking right across the wall, descending into a dry valley and climbing out the other side, passing to the south of Mas Paltré. You could turn left here and follow this track to **Cala Tavallera**, which has a super little beach; camping is possible here.

Climb the obvious path to the south-west of the beach to return to the GR11. The GR11 crosses the track and follows another heading roughly E. Pass the ruins of Mas Vell and fork right. A little later a path veers left into another dry valley and climbs out the other side. At the top, among a few stone structures just right of the trail is a stone shelter which could serve as an emergency bivouac. After a few minutes you fork left down a path, then left along a track, then you fork right – keeping a close eye on the waymarks – and eventually pass a ruined farmhouse and then an abandoned farmhouse. Keep straight on (slightly left) along a minor track and soon approach the road to **Cap de Creus**; the GR11 continues a

Hikers on Cap de Creus

bit further as a path before crossing the road (100m, **2hr**). The GR11 continues right of the road, occasionally just touching it. The well-waymarked path follows a complex route which takes you close to Cala Jugadora, which has a small sandy beach, before reaching the lighthouse (**40min**). From here follow arrows on small metal plates on the rocks to the Punta de Cap de Creus where the end of the GR11 is marked with a red and white circle on a rock (**15min**).

At Cap de Creus there is a bar-restaurant and a tapas bar, a tourist information office and toilets. There is no water point but you can ask for water at the bars. Bar-restaurant Cap de Creus, which is adjacent to the lighthouse, also offers accommodation and late-night entertainment. Given the remote location, all services are on the expensive side.

A bus service runs regularly between Cap de Creus and Cadaqués, between 8:00 and midnight.

Cadaqués, to the south-west of Cap de Creus, is a charming and popular tourist resort with hotels, shops, restaurants and beaches. At the time of writing the campground was closed and it is not clear if or when it will open again. In Port Lligat, a short distance from Cadaqués, you can visit the famous Salvador Dalí house.

Hikers with time and energy left can continue hiking from Cap de Creus on the waymarked Camí de Ronda (GR92), a coastal hiking trail, going either towards the French border or towards Barcelona.

FACILITIES ON STAGE 47

Fonda Felip: tel 972 387 271

El Port de la Selva Tourist Information Office: tel 972 387 122
www.elportdelaselva.cat

Hostal and Camping l'Arola: tel 972 387 005

Camping Port de la Selva: tel 972 387 287 www.campingselva.com

Camping Port Valley: tel 972 387 186 www.campingportdelavall.com

Hostal La Tina: tel 972 387 149 www.hostallatina.cat

Bar-restaurant Cap de Creus: tel 972 199 005
www.restaurantcapdecreus.com

Tapas bar Sa Freu: tel 619 672 710 www.restaurantbarsafreu.com

Cadaqués Tourist Information Office: tel 972 258 315
www.visitcadaques.org

APPENDIX A
Sources of information

Maps
Editorial Alpina published a set of excellent 1:50,000 maps for the GR11. The 21 maps include most but not all recent route changes and also give detailed height profiles. Note that the stage numbers differ from those in this Cicerone guide.
www.editorialalpina.com

Maps Worldwide Ltd
www.mapsworldwide.com

The Map Shop
www.themapshop.co.uk

Edward Stanford Ltd
www.stanfords.co.uk

Bibliography
Other Cicerone guides to the Pyrenees (www.cicerone.co.uk):

Pyrenean Haute Route
by Tom Martens (2019)

The GR10 Trail
by Stuart Butler (2023)

Walks and Climbs in the Pyrenees
by Kev Reynolds (2017)

Shorter Treks in the Pyrenees
by Brian Johnson (2019)

The Pyrenees
by Kev Reynolds (2010)

Walking in Catalunya - Girona Pyrenees
by Nike Werstroh and Jacint Mig (2023)

Interesting information on the GR11
www.travesiapirenaica.com/en/gr11/gr11.php
www.lasenda.net

Information on mountain refuges
Information and booking for albergues, manned and unmanned refuges in Aragón:
www.fam.es;
www.alberguesyrefugiosdearagon.com

Information and booking for refuges in Catalonia:
http://feec.cat;
www.lacentralderefugis.com;
www.refusonline.com

For tourist information and information on refuges in Andorra:
www.visitandorra.com

Travel information
Brittany Ferries
www.brittany-ferries.co.uk

National Express coaches
www.nationalexpress.com

Eurostar
www.eurostar.com

French rail network
www.sncf.com

Spanish rail network
www.renfe.com

Ryanair
www.ryanair.com

British Airways
www.britishairways.com

Air France
www.airfrance.co.uk

Easyjet
www.easyjet.com

Telephone codes
Europe-wide emergency telephone
number: 112

International telephone codes:
France +33
Spain +34
Andorra +376

Weather forecasts for the Pyrenees
www.mountain-forecast.com
www.meteoblue.com

APPENDIX B
Glossary

A = Aragón, B = Basque, C = Catalan	English	A = Aragón, B = Basque, C = Catalan	English
abri	cabin	*camino*	track
achar (A)	narrow pass	*campo*	meadow
agua	water	*can (C)*	house
aguja	needle	*canal*	narrow valley
alt, alto	high	*cap*	small hill
arroyo	stream	*capella*	chapel
avenida	avenue	*carrer (C)*	street
avinguda (C)	avenue	*carretera*	road
azul	blue	*casa*	house
baix, baxo	low	*cascada*	waterfall
balle (A)	valley	*caserio*	farm
balneario	thermal baths	*castillo*	castle
biskar (B)	shoulder	*circo*	coombe
borda	farm	*col, coll (C)*	pass
bosc (C)	wood	*colladeta*	small pass
bosque	wood	*collado*	pass
brecha	gap	*coma (A)*	coombe
caballo	horse	*creu (C)*	cross
cabana	cabin	*cuello (A)*	pass
cabezo	small hill	*embalse*	reservoir
cabo	cape	*entibo (A)*	reservoir
cala (C)	small bay	*ermita*	hermitage
calle	street	*espelunga (A)*	cave
calm (C)	bare plateau	*estación*	station

A = Aragón, B = Basque, C = Catalan	English
estany, estanh (C)	lake
estiba (A)	summer pasture
fábrica	factory
faro	lighthouse
feixa (C)	ledge
font (C)	spring
fronton (B)	pelota wall
fuén (A)	spring
fuente	spring
gran	large
hospital	hospital
hostal	small hotel
ibón (A)	lake
iturri (B)	spring
lac (A), lago	lake
llano	flat area
mas (C)	farmhouse
mendi, monte	mountain
monasterio	monastery
muga (A, B)	frontier stone
negre	black
nord	north
obago (C)	dark
orri	stone shelter
paso	pass
peña (A)	crag
pic (C)	peak
pica (C), pico	peak

A = Aragón, B = Basque, C = Catalan	English
pista	track
pla (C)	flat area
plaça	town square
plan (A)	flat area
pont (A, C)	bridge
port (C)	pass
portella	small pass
prado	meadow
puen (A)	bridge
puente	bridge
puerto	pass
puig (C)	peak
refugi (C)	mountain hut
refugio	mountain hut
regata	stream
río, riu (C)	river
san, sant (C)	saint
santa	saint
sanctuario	sanctuary
serra (C)	mountain range
sobira (C)	high
soum	rounded mountain
sud	south
torrente	mountain stream
tuc (C)	sharp summit
tuca (A, C)	sharp summit
val (A), valle	valley
vall (C)	valley

APPENDIX C
Stage Facilities Planner

Stage	Place	Altitude (m)	Walking time	Cum. Stage time	Distance (km)	Cum. distance (km)
1	**Cabo de Higuer**	**40**	-	-	-	-
1	Hondarribia	5	0hr 25	0hr 25	1.6	1.6
1	Irún	15	0hr 35	1hr	5.4	7.0
1	Ermita San Martzial	200	1hr 50	2hr 50	3.3	10.3
1	Elbalse de San Antón	240	3hr	5hr 40	10.5	20.8
1	**Bera**	**50**	**2hr 40**	**8hr 30**	**10.6**	**31.4**
2	**Elizondo**	**200**	**8hr 20**	**8hr 20**	**30.1**	**30.1**
3	**Puerto de Urkiaga**	**912**	**5hr 20**	**5hr 20**	**17.6**	**17.6**
4	Albergue Sorogain	845	2hr 20	2hr 20	7.1	7.1
4	**Burguete**	**898**	**2hr 50**	**5hr 10**	**10.1**	**17.2**
5	Orbara	767	3hr 45	3hr 45	13.7	13.7
5	*Orbaitzeta (off-route)*		*+25 min*		*1.9km*	
5	**Hiriberri**	**923**	**1hr**	**4hr 45**	**3.7**	**3.7**
6	Paso de las Alforjas	1430	4hr 45	4hr 45	12.3	12.3
6	**Ochagavia**	**770**	**2hr 5**	**6hr 50**	**8.3**	**20.6**
7	Borda de Arrese	1309	2hr 30	2hr 30	9.7	9.7
7	**Isaba**	**800**	**1hr 50**	**5hr 20**	**9.4**	**19.1**
8	**Zuriza**	**1210**	**2hr 50**	**2hr 50**	**10.8**	**10.8**
9	**La Mina**	**1230**	**4hr 20**	**4hr 20**	**11.5**	**11.5**
9A	**Puente de Santa Ana**	**930**	**6hr 15**	**6hr 15**	**18.3**	**18.3**
10	Achar d'Aguas Tuertas	1615	2hr 30	2hr 30	6.7	6.7
10	Refugio de los Forestales	1967	3hr 20	5hr 50	10.3	17
10	Refugio de Ordelca	1700	0hr 40	6hr 30	1.9	18.9
10	**Refugio de Lizara**	**1540**	**0hr 15**	**6hr 45**	**1.3**	**20.2**

⬡ hotel   ▲ mountain hut/inn   △ unmanned hut   ⬡ campsite

🍴 refreshments   ⊕ shop   ▣ train station   ▣ bus service   ⓘ information

	Facilities							
hotel	mountain hut/inn	unmanned hut	campsite	refreshments	shop	train station	bus service	information
			⬡	🍴				
⬡			⬡	🍴	⊕		▣	ⓘ
⬡				🍴	⊕	▣	▣	ⓘ
				🍴				
				🍴				
⬡				🍴	⊕		▣	ⓘ
⬡				🍴	⊕		▣	ⓘ
⬡				🍴				
⬡			⬡	🍴	⊕		▣	
				🍴				
⬡				🍴	⊕			
⬡				🍴				
		△						
⬡			⬡	🍴	⊕		▣	ⓘ
		△						
⬡				🍴	⊕		▣	ⓘ
⬡			⬡	🍴	⊕			
		△						
⬡	▲		⬡	🍴			▣	
		△						
		△						
		△						
	▲			🍴				

Stage	Place	Altitude (m)	Walking time	Cum. Stage time	Distance (km)	Cum. distance (km)
10A	Refugio de Gabardito	1363	1hr 30	1hr 30	2.5	2.5
10A	Refugio Dios Te Salbe	1550	1hr 10	2hr 40	5.4	7.9
11	**Candanchú**	**1570**	**5hr 55**	**5hr 55**	**14.8**	**14.8**
12	Área recreativa de Canal Roya	1390	0hr 50	0hr 50	3.2	3.2
12	Refugio de Lacuas	1550	0hr 45	1hr 35	2.9	6.1
12	*Formigal (off-route)*	*1500*	*+5min*		*0.5*	
12	**Sallent de Gállego**	**1295**	**5hr 05**	**6hr 40**	**17.8**	**23.9**
13	Embalse de la Serra	1438	1hr	1hr	2.5	2.5
13	**Refugio de Respomuso**	**2220**	**2hr 55**	**3hr 55**	**8.6**	**11.1**
14	Ibón Baxo de Bachimaña	2200	4hr 50	4hr 50	9	9
14	**Baños de Panticosa**	**1635**	**1hr 30**	**6hr 20**	**3.4**	**12.4**
15	Cubillar dera Labaza	1790	5hr 15	5hr 15	11.4	11.4
15	Cubillar dera Bado	1580	1hr	6hr 15	3.6	15
15	**San Nicolás de Bujaruelo**	**1338**	**1hr**	**7hr 15**	**4.9**	**19.9**
16	Camping Valle de Bujaruelo	1240	0hr 45	0hr 45	2.8	2.8
16	*Torla (off-route)*	*1020*	*+40min*		*2.8*	
16	La pradera de Ordesa	1310	2hr 45	3hr 30	9.5	12.3
16	**Refugio de Góriz**	**2160**	**4hr 25**	**7hr 55**	**12**	**24.3**
17	**Refugio de Pineta**	**1240**	**7hr 20**	**7hr 20**	**12.8**	**12.8**
18	Valle de Pineta	1290	0hr 25	0hr 25	2.2	2.2
18	Refugio Ganadero de la Estiva	2100	2hr 40	3hr 5	4.1	6.3
18	**Parzán**	**1134**	**2hr 55**	**6hr**	**13.2**	**19.5**
19	Small basic hut	1980	2hr 50	2 hr 50	9.2	9.2
19	Collado de Urdiceto	2314	0hr 55	3hr 45	2	11.2

Facilities

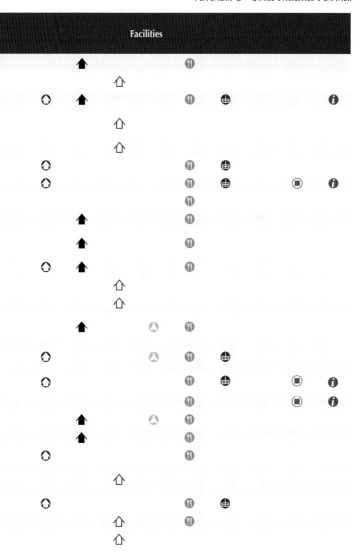

Stage	Place	Altitude (m)	Walking time	Cum. Stage time	Distance (km)	Cum. distance (km)
19	Cabana de Lisiert	1720	2hr	5hr 45	5.9	17.1
19	Camping El Forcallo	1580	0hr 30	6hr 15	2.9	20
19	**Refugio de Biadós**	**1760**	**0hr 45**	**7hr**	**1.1**	**21.1**
20	Cabana de Añescruzes	2100	1hr 40	1hr 40	3.9	3.9
20	Refugio d'Estós	1890	3hr 5	4hr 45	6.9	10.8
20	Refugio de Santa Ana	1540	1hr 25	6hr 10	6.1	16.9
20	**Puente de San Jaime**	**1250**	**0hr 35**	**6hr 45**	**3.2**	**20.1**
20	*Benasque (off-route)*	*1140*	*0hr 35*		*2.7*	
20A	**Refugio Angel Orús**	**2112**	**5hr 35**	**5hr 35**	**10.2**	**10.2**
21	Refugio d'El Quillon	1780	2hr 20	2hr 20	7.2	7.2
21	Refugio de Coronas	1960	0hr 20	2hr 40	3.1	10.3
21	**Refugio de Cap de Llauset**	**2425**	**4hr 30**	**7hr 10**	**6.6**	**16.9**
22	Refugio d'Angliós	2220	1hr 25	1hr 25	2.5	2.5
22	**Refugi de Conangles**	**1555**	**2hr 20**	**3hr45**	**7.5**	**10**
23	**Refugi dera Restanca**	**2010**	**5hr 20**	**5hr 20**	**12**	**12**
24	Cabana de Rius	1660	0hr 40	0hr 40	1.7	1.7
24	**Refugi de Colomers**	**2135**	**4hr 25**	**5hr 5**	**12.2**	**13.9**
24	*Refugi de Saboredo (off-route)*	*2300*	*+30min*		*2.2*	
25	*Refugi d'Amitges (off-route)*	*2365*	*+30min*		*1*	
25	Refugi Ernest Mallafré	1920	4hr 25	4hr 25	11.3	11.3
25	**Espot**	**1330**	**1hr 35**	**6hr**	**7.7**	**19**
26	Camping La Mola	1250	0hr 35	0hr 35	2	2
26	**La Guingueta d'Àneu**	**940**	**1hr 55**	**2hr 30**	**7.7**	**9.7**
27	**Estaon**	**1240**	**5hr 35**	**5hr 35**	**11.3**	**11.3**
28	**Tavascan**	**1120**	**4hr 15**	**4hr 15**	**12.8**	**12.8**
29	**Àreu**	**1270**	**6hr 30**	**6hr 30**	**16.7**	**16.7**

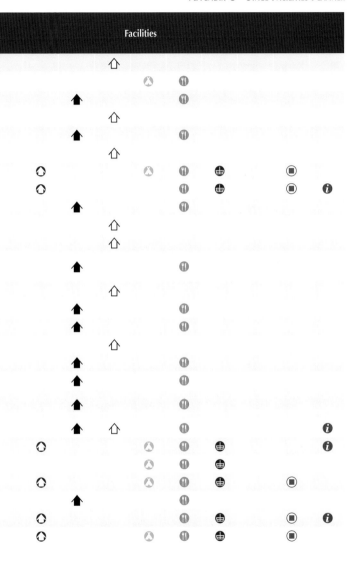

		Facilities				

Stage	Place	Altitude (m)	Walking time	Cum. Stage time	Distance (km)	Cum. distance (km)
30	**Refugi de Vallferrera**	**1920**	**3hr 20**	**3hr 20**	**10**	**10**
31	Refugi de Baiau	2517	3hr	3hr	5.9	5.9
31	**Refugi de Comapedrosa**	**2260**	**2hr 20**	**5hr 20**	**4.5**	**10.4**
32	Arinsal	1500	1hr 15	1hr 15	4	4
32	**Arans**	**1360**	**2hr 45**	**4hr**	**5.7**	**9.7**
33	La Cortinada	1330	0hr 20		1.3	
33	*Ordino (off-route)*	*1300*	*+15min*		*0.8*	
33	**Encamp**	**1270**	**6hr**	**6hr**	**14.9**	**14.9**
34	Refugi de Fontverd	1890	3hr 25	3hr 25	8.8	8.8
34	Refugi Riu dels Orris	2230	1hr 25	4hr 50	4.2	13
34	**Refugi de l'Illa**	**2485**	**0hr 55**	**5hr 45**	**2.8**	**15.8**
35	Cabana dels Espavers	2068	1hr 20	1hr 20	4.5	4.5
35	Refugi Engorgs	2380	2hr 35	3hr 55	4.9	9.4
35	**Refugi de Malniu**	**2138**	**1hr 40**	**5hr 35**	**4.9**	**14.3**
36	Refugi de la Feixa	2160	0hr 40	0hr 40	2.8	2.8
36	Guils de Cerdanya	1380	0hr 55	1hr 35	5.8	8.6
36	Saneja	1220	1hr 5	2hr 40	2.6	11.2
36	**Puigcerda**	**1204**	**0hr 30**	**3hr 10**	**3**	**14.2**
37	Age	1150	0hr 25	0hr 25	2.1	2.1
37	**Camping Can Fosses / Planoles**	**1260**	**6hr 25**	**6hr 50**	**25**	**27.1**
38	Refugi Corral Blanc	1820	1hr 25	1hr 25	2.3	2.3
38	Queralbs	1196	2hr 5	3hr 30	7.8	10.1
38	**Núria**	**1967**	**2hr 55**	**6hr 25**	**8.1**	**18.2**
39	Refugi d'Ulldeter	2220	4hr 15	4hr 15	11.5	11.5
39	Hostal Pastuira	1990	0hr 25	4hr 40	1.3	12.8
39	**Setcases**	**1265**	**1hr 20**	**6hr**	**6.9**	**19.7**
40	Molló	1184	3hr 25	3hr 25	11.5	11.5

Facilities

Stage	Place	Altitude (m)	Walking time	Cum. Stage time	Distance (km)	Cum. distance (km)
40	Casa Etxalde	1020	1hr 15	4hr 40	5.3	16.8
40	**Beget**	**540**	**1hr 40**	**6hr 20**	**6.5**	**23.3**
41	Talaixa	760	3hr 35	3hr 35	12.1	12.1
41	**Sant Aniol d'Aguja**	**450**	**0hr 50**	**4hr 25**	**3.6**	**15.7**
42	Refugi de Bassegoda	820	3hr 15	3hr 15	7.9	7.9
42	**Albanya**	**237**	**1hr 55**	**5hr 10**	**10.3**	**18.2**
43	*Camping Maçanet de Cabrenys (off-route)*	*370*	*0hr 15*		*1km*	
43	**Maçanet de Cabrenys**	**350**	**4hr 45**	**4hr 45**	**19.7**	**19.7**
44	La Vajol	530	1hr 50	1hr 50	8.1	8.1
44	**La Jonquera**	**114**	**3hr 20**	**5hr 10**	**15**	**23.1**
45	Requesens	500	3hr 20	3hr 20	11.1	11.1
45	**Els Vilars**	**220**	**3hr 15**	**6hr 35**	**14**	**25.1**
46	Sant Quirze de Colera	165	2hr 25	2hr 25	10.4	10.4
46	Vilamaniscle	155	1hr 10	3hr 35	5.6	16
46	**Llançà**	**10**	**1hr 55**	**5hr 30**	**10.1**	**26.1**
46A	Espolla	130	0hr 30	0hr 30	2.3	2.3
46A	Rabos	116	0hr 55	0hr 55	3.5	5.8
47	Sant Pere de Rodes	520	2hr 5	2hr 5	6.3	6.3
47	La Selva de Mar	50	0hr 45	2hr 40	2.6	8.9
47	El Port de la Selva	5	0hr 45	3hr 25	2.4	11.3
47	**Cap de Creus**	**10**	**4hr 10**	**7hr 35**	**16.4**	**27.7**

Facilities

NOTES

NOTES

NOTES

NOTES

DOWNLOAD THE GPX FILES

All the routes in this guide are available for download from:

www.cicerone.co.uk/1166/GPX

as standard format GPX files. You should be able to load them into most online GPX systems and mobile devices, whether GPS or smartphone. You may need to convert the file into your preferred format using a conversion programme such as gpsvisualizer.com or one of the many other such websites and programmes.

When you follow this link, you will be asked for your email address and where you purchased the guidebook, and have the option to subscribe to the Cicerone e-newsletter.

www.cicerone.co.uk

LISTING OF CICERONE GUIDES

BRITISH ISLES CHALLENGES, COLLECTIONS AND ACTIVITIES

Cycling Land's End to John o' Groats
Great Walks on the England Coast Path
The Big Rounds
The Book of the Bivvy
The Book of the Bothy
The Mountains of England and Wales: Vol 1 Wales
The Mountains of England and Wales: Vol 2 England
The National Trails
Walking the End to End Trail

SHORT WALKS SERIES

Short Walks Hadrian's Wall
Short Walks in Arnside and Silverdale
Short Walks in Cornwall: Falmouth and the Lizard
Short Walks in Dumfries and Galloway
Short Walks in Nidderdale
Short Walks in Pembrokeshire: Tenby and the south
Short Walks in the South Downs: Brighton, Eastbourne and Arundel
Short Walks in the Surrey Hills
Short Walks Lake District – Coniston and Langdale
Short Walks Lake District: Keswick, Borrowdale and Buttermere
Short Walks Lake District: Windermere Ambleside and Grasmere
Short Walks on the Malvern Hills
Short Walks Winchester

SCOTLAND

Ben Nevis and Glen Coe
Cycling in the Hebrides
Cycling the North Coast 500
Great Mountain Days in Scotland
Mountain Biking in Southern and Central Scotland
Mountain Biking in West and North West Scotland
Not the West Highland Way
Scotland
Scotland's Best Small Mountains
Scotland's Mountain Ridges
Scottish Wild Country Backpacking
Skye's Cuillin Ridge Traverse
The Borders Abbeys Way
The Great Glen Way
The Great Glen Way Map Booklet
The Hebridean Way
The Hebrides
The Isle of Mull
The Isle of Skye
The Skye Trail

The Southern Upland Way
The West Highland Way
The West Highland Way Map Booklet
Walking Ben Lawers, Rannoch and Atholl
Walking in the Cairngorms
Walking in the Pentland Hills
Walking in the Scottish Borders
Walking in the Southern Uplands
Walking in Torridon, Fisherfield, Fannichs and An Teallach
Walking Loch Lomond and the Trossachs
Walking on Arran
Walking on Harris and Lewis
Walking on Jura, Islay and Colonsay
Walking on Rum and the Small Isles
Walking on the Orkney and Shetland Isles
Walking on Uist and Barra
Walking the Cape Wrath Trail
Walking the Corbetts
  Vol 1 South of the Great Glen
  Vol 2 North of the Great Glen
Walking the Galloway Hills
Walking the John o' Groats Trail
Walking the Munros
  Vol 1 – Southern, Central and Western Highlands
  Vol 2 – Northern Highlands and the Cairngorms
Winter Climbs in the Cairngorms
Winter Climbs: Ben Nevis and Glen Coe

NORTHERN ENGLAND ROUTES

Cycling the Reivers Route
Cycling the Way of the Roses
Hadrian's Cycleway
Hadrian's Wall Path
Hadrian's Wall Path Map Booklet
The Coast to Coast Cycle Route
The Coast to Coast Walk
The Coast to Coast Walk Map Booklet
The Pennine Way
The Pennine Way Map Booklet
Walking the Dales Way
Walking the Dales Way Map Booklet

NORTH-EAST ENGLAND, YORKSHIRE DALES AND PENNINES

Cycling in the Yorkshire Dales
Great Mountain Days in the Pennines
Mountain Biking in the Yorkshire Dales
The Cleveland Way and the Yorkshire Wolds Way
The North York Moors

Trail and Fell Running in the Yorkshire Dales
Walking in County Durham
Walking in Northumberland
Walking in the North Pennines
Walking in the Yorkshire Dales: North and East
  South and West
Walking St Cuthbert's Way
Walking St Oswald's Way and Northumberland Coast Path

NORTH-WEST ENGLAND AND THE ISLE OF MAN

Cycling the Pennine Bridleway
Isle of Man Coastal Path
The Lancashire Cycleway
The Lune Valley and Howgills
Walking in Cumbria's Eden Valley
Walking in Lancashire
Walking in the Forest of Bowland and Pendle
Walking on the Isle of Man
Walking on the West Pennine Moors
Walking the Ribble Way
Walks in Silverdale and Arnside

LAKE DISTRICT

Bikepacking in the Lake District
Cycling in the Lake District
Great Mountain Days in the Lake District
Joss Naylor's Lakes, Meres and Waters of the Lake District
Lake District Winter Climbs
Lake District:
  High Level and Fell Walks
  Low Level and Lake Walks
Mountain Biking in the Lake District
Outdoor Adventures with Children – Lake District
Scrambles in the Lake District –
  North
  South
Trail and Fell Running in the Lake District
Walking The Cumbria Way
Walking the Lake District Fells –
  Borrowdale
  Buttermere
  Coniston
  Keswick
  Langdale
  Mardale and the Far East
  Patterdale
  Wasdale
Walking the Tour of the Lake District

DERBYSHIRE, PEAK DISTRICT AND MIDLANDS

Cycling in the Peak District
Dark Peak Walks
Scrambles in the Dark Peak

For full information on all our
guides, books and eBooks,
visit our website:
www.cicerone.co.uk

CICERONE

Trust Cicerone to guide your next adventure,
wherever it may be around the world...

Discover guides for hiking, mountain walking, backpacking,
trekking, trail running, cycling and mountain biking, ski touring,
climbing and scrambling in Britain, Europe and worldwide.

Connect with Cicerone online and find inspiration.

- buy books and ebooks
- articles, advice and trip reports
- podcasts and live events
- GPX files and updates
- regular newsletter

cicerone.co.uk